Birdwatching

Birdwatching

Tips, Techniques, and Equipment
for Understanding and Observing Birds

Dr. Janann V. Jenner

Introduction by Christine Sheppard

FRIEDMAN/FAIRFAX
PUBLISHERS

A FRIEDMAN/FAIRFAX BOOK

Library of Congress Cataloging-in-Publication Data

Jenner, Janann V.
     [Birdwatcher's companion]
     Birdwatching : tips, techniques, and equipment for
     understanding and observing birds / by Janann V. Jenner.
          p.   cm.
     "Originally published as The birdwatchers companion"
     --T.p. verso.
     Includes bibliographical references (p.   ) and index.
     ISBN 1-56799-277-3 (HC)
     1. Bird watching.   2. Birds.   I. Title.
QL677.5.J46 1996   95-52698
598'.07234--dc20   CIP

Editor: Sharyn Rosart
Art Director: Jeff Batzli
Designer: Barbara Gold
Photography Editors: Anne K. Price and Emilya Naymark
Production Associate: Camille Lee

Originally published as *The Birdwatcher's Companion.*

Color separations by Ocean Graphic International
Company Limited
Printed in China by Leefung-Asco Printers Ltd.

For bulk purchases and special sales, please contact:
Friedman/Fairfax Publishers
Attention: Sales Department
15 West 26th Street
New York, New York 10010
212/685-6610 FAX 212/685-1307

Acknowledgments

*The author wishes to thank H. G. Dowling, Peg Summers,
Miesje Jolley, and Norman Levine, who criticized the manuscript
and offered comments and encouragement.*

Dedication

*I have been fortunate in studying under many fine teachers and
this book is affectionately dedicated to two of them.*

*Isabel Johnson was my zoology teacher at Chicago's
Carl Schurz High School. Her classes were always my favorites
and she had a larger-than-life mystique that transformed desiccated, preserved
jellyfishes and lampreys into fascinating creatures.
Thank you, Miss Johnson, wherever you are.*

*Herndon G. Dowling of the Biology Department at
New York University is an inspiration to all of his graduate students.
His knowledge of herpetology is legendary and I am honored to have
been associated with his laboratory. More than anyone else,
H. G. D. has taught me how to be a field biologist.*

PHOTO CREDITS

Courtesy of the American Museum of Natural History: pp. 9, 12 bottom, 14,
15; © **Christopher Bain**: p. 63; © **Richard Day**: pp. 6, 27 top right, 33, 39, 41
bottom, 42, 49, 53, 54, 58, 61, 62, 67, 75, 77, 82, 87, 96, 104, 105, 106, 107, 111,
113; © **Susan Day**: p. 85; **Envision**: © Gary Crandall: pp. 38, 48, 99, 122;
© Grace Davies: p. 78; © MacDonald: pp. 47 right, 115; © Ellen Sandberg: pp. 92,
93; **FPG International**: © Michael Rothwell: p. 109; © **Michael Francis**:
p. 65; © **Neal and Molly Jansen**: p. 72; © **Maslowski Wildlife Productions**:
pp. 24, 69, 88, 108; **Photobank, Inc.**: © Bob Jacobson: p. 30 left; © Lee Peterson:
p. 17; © Larry Mulvehill: p. 29; © Nancy Sams: p. 91; © **Anthony V. Smith**:
p. 97; **Tom Stack and Associates**: © Mary Clay: p. 81; © Mark Clay: p. 44 left;
© Jeff Foott: p. 84; © John Gerlach: pp. 18, 27 top left, 66; © Kerry T. Givens:
p. 70; © Thomas Kitchin: pp. 41 top, 43, 44 right, 94, 95, 102, 119, 120;
© Gary Milburn: p. 110; © Rod Planck: pp. 2, 64, 100; © Milton Rand: pp. 26;
© Shatil/Rozinsky: pp. 52, 101; © John Shaw: pp. 11, 89; © Diana L. Stratton:
pp. 35, 60; © Roy Toft: p. 55; © Dave Watts: p. 112; © **Illustrations by Van Der
Steelink**: pp. 10, 25, 27 bottom, 28, 32, 34, 37, 40, 47 left; **Visuals Unlimited**:
© Tom Ulrich: p. 71; **The Wildlife Collection**: © Martin Harvey: p. 12 top;
© Michael Francis: p. 59; © Henry Holdsworth: pp. 57, 68; © Robert Lankinen:
pp. 36, 46, 116; ©Charles Melton: pp. 16, 90; © Clay Myers: p. 30 right

INTRODUCTION

I can't prove it, but I believe that birdwatching is at least as old as humanity. Perhaps people began watching birds because birds and their eggs are good to eat. However, birds also tell a lot about what is happening in an environment, and the earliest birdwatchers were practicing survival skills. Birds can warn of predators and help spot food sources, as well as forecast changes in the weather, the turn of seasons, and possibly even volcanic eruptions. Even today, people who live in the rain forests of New Guinea or Brazil know the birds of their region, just as we know how to drive a car or any other skill that helps us get along in our environment. They know where to find a Screaming Pitohui, what a Parotia eats, the reasons to follow a Honeyguide, and what it means if an Antbird suddenly flies across the trail. Most city dwellers don't learn these lessons of nature in such detail, but they may still know that the first Robin means that spring has come and that flights of Geese signal the end of summer.

Watching birds is one of the easiest ways for people to approach nature. Most birds are active during the day, and you don't need to go anywhere special to find a variety of species. Whether you live in Alaska or Florida, there are birds in nearby parks, in the trees behind your house, or at the local dump. If you watch in the same area every day, you will probably begin to recognize the feathered residents of your neighborhood as well as spot transients.

Even the most common bird has its own story and history. As you watch birds, you'll begin to realize how much their lives resemble ours, centering on the need for security, food, shelter, and a mate. Far from being the carefree creatures we imagine, birds live serious lives. Rather than flitting about randomly, they usually settle in a specific area, because knowledge of their environment is key to survival. Simply watching birds at a backyard feeder can initiate you into the complexity of bird life. Different species and individuals have varying ranks in the backyard society and may chase others or be chased from the feeder.

Birdwatching is one of the best family activities, for it appeals to both parents and children—no matter what their level of knowledge and skill—and provides entertainment and exercise as well as education. Setting up and watching a feeder, taking children to see ducks at the park, and counting the number of bird species spotted on a drive are all good activities for new birders. As the family grows more experienced at birdwatching, they may add birding to camping, cycling, and canoe trips.

Even casual birding is endlessly rewarding, though many birdwatchers find that their interest grows to near-obsession. For some, the challenge of adding new species to the list of those already seen can become almost a competitive sport. Finding birds can be a reason to explore new habitats and new places. While most birders are content with binoculars and notebooks, a few adventurous types use gliders or light aircraft to meet birds on the wing or trek into uninhabited areas to spot an elusive species.

Another of birdwatching's pluses is that it can be enjoyed year-round. The birds in an area may change with the season—pairing off to breed, flocking to migrate, or moving to exploit new food sources—but every season has birds, and they respond to habitat changes with different kinds of behavior. In the north, spring and summer bring migrant species that arrive to breed, establish territories, court, nest, and rear their young. Winter shows how well adapted to tough habitats birds can be, as they forage for hard-to-find foods and fly in even the most bitter weather.

While birding requires no training or equipment, a pair of binoculars and a bit of coaching can add significantly to the experience. *Birdwatching* is designed to provide the basics for beginners but will make a good reference for birders of almost any level. The book provides an excellent overview of bird biology, written clearly and simply but not simplistically. You'll learn how the special structure of feathers keeps birds warm and dry, and how feather colors are produced. Birds have a long and fairly complex evolution, and you'll discover the debate over the origin of flight and the biological trade-offs birds made to master the air.

For the birdwatcher just getting started, there are simple suggestions that will pay off over a lifetime. Carrying a pencil and notebook seems basic enough, but these aren't the first things most novice birders would think to bring. Thorough discussions tell you how to find birds, what kinds of bird books to look for, and how to buy binoculars, providing basic information that can otherwise be hard to come by. My favorite section deals with watching pigeons, birds that many of us tend to ignore because they are so commonplace. Observing these ubiquitous birds provides valuable practice in using binoculars, recognizing individuals, identifying behaviors and interactions, and taking notes. We come to realize that common does not imply dull and that literally any bird can be worth watching.

Birdwatching is a book that birders will turn to again and again. The compact course in ornithology and the references are sure to be consulted repeatedly, while the technical information about binoculars and scopes guides birders as they advance in expertise and acquire new equipment.

Of the more than nine thousand species of birds, at least one thousand species are endangered and nearly that many are at serious risk. Habitat destruction—for agriculture, mining, construction, and other uses—is the primary cause of declining populations. Some destruction, like draining marshes and cutting trees, is intentional. Other problems—including oil spills and poisoning of water supplies by pesticides—may be accidental but are no less devastating.

Birds have always been part of our mythology; they are symbols of freedom, fidelity, courage, and joy. By watching birds, we understand how these feathered creatures came to represent our own most precious attributes. We should also learn that losing birds is both a loss and a warning to us, since we share their world and will ultimately share their fate.

Christine Sheppard
Curator of Ornithology
Wildlife Conservation Society

CHAPTER 1

Bird Evolution

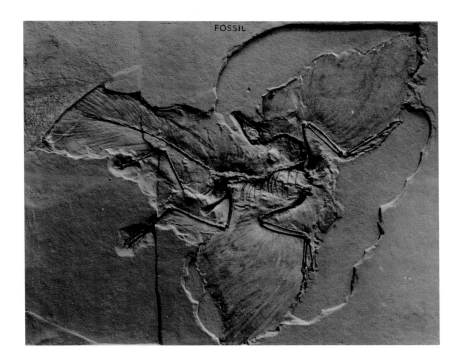

FOSSIL

*I*n 1861, Herman von Meyer, a Bavarian quarry worker, spotted a feather in a slab of limestone and thus found one of the most significant fossils known to paleontology. The finely grained, high-quality limestone quarried in southern Germany was intended to be used to print lithographs, which were all the rage in the 1800s. Limestone is quarried in large slabs, and prior to sale, the slabs are split and carefully inspected for imperfections that will spoil an artist's work. Meyer was a fossil hunter and amateur paleontologist as well as a quarryman. He realized that a prehistoric bird must have dropped the feather now visible as a blackened imprint in the rock; he also knew that no one had ever found a fossil bird. So, Meyer began an excited search of other slabs of limestone for the entire animal. A month later, in a second quarry not far from the original site, he found what he was looking for: a skeleton with the clear imprint of feathers. He gave it the memorable scientific name, *Archaeopteryx lithographica,* Latin for "ancient, winged thing found in lithographic limestone." The fossil subsequently changed hands several times and now is in the collection of the British Museum.

Since the discovery of these two fossils, only three other specimens of *Archaeopteryx* have been found, all from the limestone quarries in Bavaria. But even though "bird paleontologists" have only four feathered skeletons (in various states of preservation) and Meyer's single, fossilized feather from *Archaeopteryx,* they do know that this creature was flying when Jurassic dinosaurs such as *Ultrasaurus* and *Stegosaurus* were lumbering about the continents.

FEATHERY EVIDENCE

You might wonder how we are certain that *Archaeopteryx* flew when no human was around to observe. The answer, expounded in detail in *The Age of Birds* by Alan Feduccia, is clearly visible in the imprints of *Archaeopteryx's* feathers, but to understand it, we have to look at the feathers of living birds.

As you would expect from their name, flight feathers are found on wings; they are one kind of contour feather, the technical name for feathers that give shape to a bird's body. Primary feathers, the largest flight feathers, are attached to the skin and bones of the

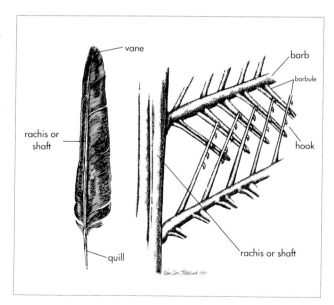

The vane of a flight feather is composed of a row of closely set barbs attached to a central rachis, or feather shaft. Each barb has rows of barbules that hook together. Interlocking barbules create the flat vane: a strong, flexible, lightweight airfoil. When birds preen their feathers, their bills zip the hooked barbules together.

wrist and hand. Most perching birds (called passerines) have nine functional primaries on each wing, and most nonperching birds have ten. Grebes, storks, and flamingos are an exception; they have eleven primaries on each wing. Smaller flight feathers, called secondaries, are associated with the forearm or ulna. Although hummingbirds, with six, and albatrosses, with forty, are extremes, most birds have between ten and twenty secondaries.

If you compare a contour feather from a Screech Owl's breast—or from its head, back, tail, or thighs—with one of the primary or secondary feathers from its wings, the difference is obvious: Flight feathers are asymmetrical; other contour feathers are symmetrical. It is equally revealing to make a three-way comparison between the primaries of birds that fly, such as the Turkey Vulture, American Kestrel, or European Starling, and birds that have a long history of flightlessness, such as the ostrich or rhea, and, finally, of birds that have only recently (geologically speaking) given up flight for a terrestrial existence, such as Hawaiian flightless rails. The feathers give a clear indication of whether a bird flies or not. Furthermore, because the smaller vane faces into the wind and the larger vane trails behind (making each feather a miniature airfoil), each flight feather tells whether it belonged to a left or right wing. Thus, we can conclude that Meyer's fossilized feather fell from the right wing of *Archaeopteryx lithographica* some 160 million years ago.

Close study of *Archaeopteryx* shows that although "Ancient Wing" had feathers and could fly, it also had many features that are more characteristic of reptiles than modern birds. These include teeth, a trailing tail supported by many vertebrae, and claws on the hind limbs and forelimbs. It does share some characteristics with modern birds, notably forelimbs modified into wings, scales modified into feathers, and collarbones fused into a wishbone (technically termed a furcula). The chart below compares birds, reptiles, and Archaeopteryx. Clearly, Ancient Wing was a kind of bird, but anatomically it was quite different from modern birds. It may have been a

The color of Ring-necked Pheasant feathers results from pigments deposited within the feathers, while the iridescence is caused by structural disruptions of the surface.

Left: *Contour feathers of emus (Dromaius novaehollandiae) have no barb-and-barbule mechanism, so they are soft and limp. Emus are flightless.*

Below: *An artist's concept of how Archaeopteryx lithographica might have looked shortly after it died in the lagoon that eventually became Bavarian limestone. Note its un-bird-like teeth, the claws on its wings, and its long tail.*

bird-reptile, a reptile-bird, or a proto-bird, but it could fly, though perhaps only weakly. *Archaeopteryx* may have been a branch runner like the African turacos, or it may have been the Jurassic ecological equivalent of a roadrunner: a bird that raced and flapped along the ground, snatching insects and lizard-sized dinosaurs in its beak.

The illustration at right is one artist's conception of how *Archaeopteryx* might have looked in breeding plumage. Did it sing? Did it brood pin-feathered nestlings? Unfortunately, the answers to these questions may never be answered by the rocks.

RESTORATION

A Comparison of Characteristics

	BIRDS	ARCHAEOPTERYX	REPTILES
Feathers	yes	yes	no
Scales	yes, on feet	yes, on feet	yes, on entire body
Forelimbs winged	yes	yes	no
Digits	reduced	reduced	5-fingered
Claws on wings	no, except hoatzin	yes	yes
Claws on feet	yes	yes	yes
Tail	tail reduced	long, bony tail	long, bony tail
Teeth	none	many	many
Bony eye ring	yes	yes	yes
Keel on sternum	yes, except ratites	no	no
Furcula	yes	yes	no, except coelurosaurs
Large brain	yes	no	no
Pneumatic bones	yes	no	no
Shelled eggs	yes	?	yes
Eggtooth	yes	?	yes

Who Were Its Ancestors?   Without its feathers, *Archaeopteryx* looks like a small, bipedal dinosaur. The skeleton is so reptilelike that two *Archaeopteryx* fossils with feathers only barely visible were once misidentified, one as a dinosaur and the other as a flying reptile (a pterosaur). Much later, their true nature was discovered by paleontologists studying museum collections. While *Archaeopteryx* provides clear evidence that birds arose from reptiles, the question remains: Which reptiles were the ancestors of birds?

There are two schools of thought. Some experts suggest a group of small, bipedal reptiles called pseudosuchians, because of similarities in the skulls, limb bones, shoulder and hip girdles, and tail vertebrae. Other experts place emphasis on the wishbone, or furcula, and suggest the coelurosaurs, a separate group of small bipedal dinosaurs, as the ancestral stock. This debate will not be resolved until more protoavian fossils are unearthed.

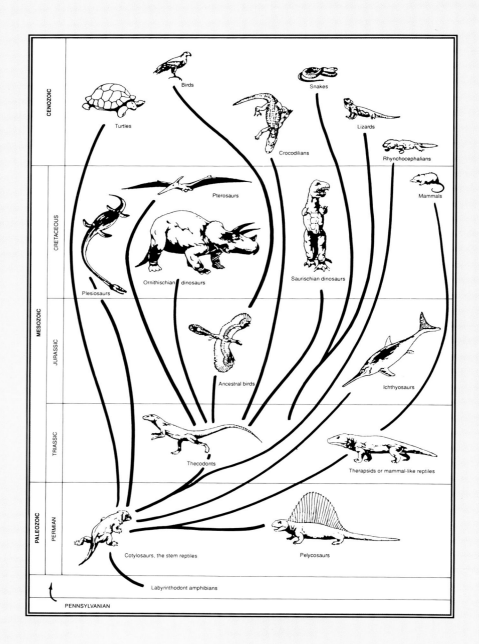

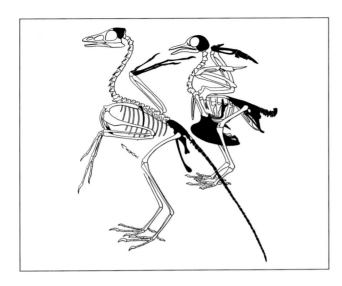

Opposite: *One theory of the origin of birds traces them back in time to Triassic thecodonts, a group of lightly built, bipedal reptiles that also gave rise to the pterosaurs, the ornithischian and saurischian dinosaurs, and the crocodiles. An alternate theory (not shown here) derives the birds from the coelurosaurs: small, agile, bipedal dinosaurs. Whatever their origin, the ancestral, reptilian body architecture and physiology have been drastically overhauled to allow birds to fly.*

Left: *Like modern birds, Archaeopteryx has a furcula and fore-limbs modified into wings. Unlike modern flying birds, Archaeopteryx has a flat sternum, a long, bony tail, and claws on its wings.*

LATIN NAMES

There is no escaping them. Any discussion of taxonomy, classification, or evolution involves the use of Latin names and long words with Greek and Latin roots. If you are unfamiliar with this lingo, it can be discouraging; but if you like a mystery and are willing to hunt for clues, Latin names and terminology can be intriguing and even addictive puzzles.

There are many rules and much fussing over the proper pronunciation of Latin words. Scientists with British and Continental schooling despair over the unpolished way many North Americans mangle Latin; North Americans with East Coast training speak a different brand of Latin from those from the West; no one is sure what the Australians are doing, but it is unique. To my way of thinking, this wrangling is a tempest in an ivory-towered teapot; if you are a beginner, try to pronounce Latin terms as best you can and to improve as you learn more. Here are two suggestions to make this easier:

• **Say everything**. Until someone corrects you, pronounce all vowels, all consonants, and all syllables. Consider, for example, the name of the Black-headed Gull, *Larus ridibundus*. Most Americans will pronounce the first name (or genus) as "la-rus," but "lay-rus" and "lah-rus" are acceptable. Pronounce all the syllables of the second name (technically called the specific epithet);

it should come out something like "rid-e-bun-dus." The accent should be on the penultimate syllable (the one preceding the last).

- **Understand how to use Latin names**. A few rules, though somewhat tricky, govern the correct written usage of Latin names. These rules are nearly universally misunderstood by non-biologists, and when you have mastered them, you will be able to see how baffled most of the world is by Latin names.

Each species is assigned a two-word name, technically called a binomial (Latin for "two names"). The international rules for nomenclature dictate that only one species of animal or plant can have a particular binomial. Humans' scientific name is *Homo sapiens*. This much is simple; here comes the tricky part: What is the name for our species? If you are thinking sapiens, you are only half-right, because a binomial must have two terms. *Homo sapiens* is the correct name for our species; anything else is wrong. In print, once the genus has been used and thus identified to the reader, it can be subsequently abbreviated, for example, *H. sapiens*.

The genus is always capitalized while the specific epithet is never capitalized. Both words are underlined or italicized in print because they are Latin.

Now that you have mastered binomials, the fun of Latin names begins. Latin names are descriptive, often poetic, and sometimes funny; searching for their meanings in a dictionary will give an added dimension to your understanding of a bird species. For example, once you know that the Belted Kingfisher is *Megaceryle alcyon*, which literally means "big, blue kingfisher," you can discover that the

The genus name for the Blue Jay (Cyanocitta cristata) comes from the Greek words for blue, kyanos, and for jay, kitta. The species name is derived from the Latin crista, which means "crested."

The cormorant genus, Phalacrocorax, is named for the Greek word for cormorant, phalakrokorax, coined from "bald" (phalakros) and "raven" (korax). Black plumage probably accounts for the raven designation; the reference to baldness is more obscure. The specific name for the Double Crested Cormorant, Phalacrocorax auritus, is from auris, Latin for "ear" and probably refers to the tufts or crests on the crown of the head.

Latin word, *alcyon*, also means calm and peaceful.

Alcyon comes from the Greek word for kingfisher. It is a two-part compound word: *(h)als*, meaning the sea, and *kuo (cyon)*, meaning to brood on. The Ancient Greeks and Sicilians believed that kingfishers nested at sea about the time of the winter solstice and that during its incubation, the kingfisher had mythic power to calm the waves. Thus halcyon means a calm and peaceful period. Whenever I think of the kingfisher, I remember Shakespeare's reference to summer's halcyon days (in King Henry VI) and imagine a warm afternoon, a cloudless blue sky, sunlight filtering through willow leaves—and the rattle from a bundle of blue feathers that hovers over a still pond. Given this somewhat elaborate mental hook, I find *Megaceryle alcyon* easy to remember.

What Do They Mean?   Some Latin names are onomatopoeic and mimic the call of a bird: Thus, the Corncrake is *Crex crex* and the Great Horned Owl is *Bubo bubo*. Some comment on the appearance of a bird: Thus, *Cyannocitta cristata* means "Blue jay with a crest" and perfectly describes the Blue Jay. Some names hint at habits: *Melospiza melodia* (literally "melodious song-finch") sets the Song Sparrow apart from the other, less tuneful, sparrows. Some names describe the geographic range of the species or tell the place where it was first collected: *Buteo jamaicensis* is the Red-tailed Hawk, a species first collected on the island of Jamaica. (It ranges from Alaska south to Panama as well as being present on Haiti, Puerto Rico, and the Virgin Islands.) The Mourning Warbler, *Oporornis philadelphia*, is literally "a bird passing through Philadelphia." The name presumably describes an individual collected on migration.

Names like *Vireo belli*, *Myadestes townsendi*, and *Thryomanes bewickii* (Bell's Vireo, Townsend's Solitaire, and Bewick's Wren, respectively) commemorate notable ornithologists and bird enthusiasts. *Pygoscelis adelie*, the Adélie Penguin, was named for the wife of the Antarctic explorer who first described it. Finally, some Latin names incorporate local or dialectical names: *Upupa epops* is the Hoopoe; *Tauraco schuttii* is the Blackbilled Touraco.

Handy Endings   In a taxonomic arrangement of birds, a hierarchical ranking system is used to attempt to impose order on the more than 9,021 species. Similar species are grouped into a genus; similar genera are grouped into a family; similar families are grouped into an order. All orders are grouped into Class Aves, informally known as birds. Class Aves has equivalent rank to

TEST YOURSELF

If you can find five mistakes in the examples below you will have learned the basics of binomial nomenclature (answers are at the end of the chapter).

canis familiaris

Equus caballus

Felis Domesticus

Mus Musculus

Bos taurus

An American Bittern stalks through marsh grasses in North Dakota. Known to science as Botaurus lentiginosus, "freckled heron," the American Bittern has many common names that refer to its un-bird-like song. Some say that its deep, "whonk-a-chonk, whonk-a-chonk, whonk-a-chonk" sounds like someone is using a plunger to open a clogged drain. To me it sounds like a lovesick sump pump.

other classes of vertebrates such as Reptilia, Mammalia, Amphibia, Chondrichthyes, Osteichthyes, and Agnatha.

Unlike binomials, the Latin names of higher taxons (from family to class) are never underlined or italicized. They are usually capitalized. Family names are identified by the Latin suffix *-idae* (meaning "family") attached to the name of the most representative or first-described genus in the family. For example, jacanas, long-toed wading birds of the Neotropics, are placed in Family Jacanidae; rheas, the South American equivalent of the ostrich, are placed in Family Rheidae; pelicans are placed in Family Pelecanidae.

Names of orders are formed by adding the suffix *-iformes* (Latin for "shape") to the most representative genus. Using our same examples, we have Order Charadriiformes, which includes all wading birds (Charadriidae is the family of the plovers); Order Rheiformes, which contains the two living rheas as well as all the extinct forms; and Order Pelecaniformes, which encompasses pelicans as well as their relatives—boobies, shags, gannets, cormorants, anhingas, and tropic birds.

> ## ANSWERS TO LATIN NAMES QUIZ:
>
> *Canis familiaris*   (dog)
> *Equus caballus*   (horse)
> *Felis domesticus*   (cat)
> *Mus musculus*   (mouse)
> *Bos taurus*   (bull)

CLASSIFICATION

Classification attempts to arrange living things in a way that reflects both their relationships to one another and their evolutionary history. It is a highly volatile and controversial science that only recently is beginning to use molecular evidence as a basis for deciding what is related to what. Up until twenty years ago, classification was mostly based on similarities in body shape. But, because the environment often shapes two distantly related groups of birds in a similar way if they are doing similar things, relying on structure alone can lead to errors in classification. The table on pages 20 to 23 follows the ideas of many taxonomists as presented by Gill (1990). Because taxonomists are constantly studying groups of birds and tinkering with classifications, trying to elucidate relationships, this listing may be out of date by the time you read it, but it will still give you an idea of how the species of birds are related to one another.

Classification of Living Birds

Order Tinamiformes—tinamous (1 family; 47 species)

    Family Tinamidae—tinamous (47 species)

Order Rheiformes—rheas (1 family; 2 species)

    Family Rheidae—rheas (2 species)

Order Struthioniformes—ostriches (1 family; 1 species)

    Family Struthionidae—ostriches (1 species)

Order Casuariiformes—cassowaries and emus
(2 families; 5 species)

    Family Dromiceiidae—emus (2 species)

    Family Casuariidae—cassowaries (3 species)

Order Dinornithiformes—kiwis (1 family; 1–5 species)

    Family Podicipedidae—grebes (21 species)

Order Podicipediformes—grebes (1 family; 21 species)

    Family Podicipedidae—grebes (21 species)

Order Sphenisciformes—penguins (1 family; 18 species)

    Family Spheniscidae—penguins (18 species)

Order Procellariiformes—albatrosses and allies
(4 families; 104 species)

    Family Diomedeidae—albatrosses (13 species)

    Family Procellariidae—shearwaters (66 species)

    Family Hydrobatidae—storm petrels (21 species)

    Family Pelecanoididae—diving petrels (4 species)

Order Pelecaniformes—pelicans, gannets, and
cormorants (6 families; 62 species)

    Family Phaëthontidae—tropic birds (3 species)

    Family Fregatidae—frigatebirds (5 species)

    Family Sulidae—boobies and gannets (9 species)

    Family Phalacrocoracidae—cormorants (33 species)

    Family Anhingidae—tropical darters or snakebirds
(4 species)

    Family Pelecanidae—pelicans (8 species)

Order Anseriformes—waterfowl (2 families; 150 species)

    Family Anhimidae—screamers (3 species)

    Family Anatidae—ducks, geese, and swans
(147 species)

Order Phoenicopteriformes—flamingos (6 species)

    Family Phoenicopteridae—flamingos (6 species)

Order Ciconiiformes—long-legged waders (5 families;
120 species)

    Family Ardeidae—herons, egrets, and bitterns
(62 species)

    Family Balaenicipitidae—whale-headed stork
(1 species)

    Family Scopidae—hammerhead (1 species)

    Family Threskiornithidae—ibises and spoonbills
(33 species)

    Family Ciconiidae—wood ibises and storks
(17 species)

Order Falconiformes—hawks, eagles, and falcons
(5 families; 288 species)

    Family Cathartidae—New World vultures
(7 species)

    Family Sagittariidae—secretary bird (1 species)

    Family Accipitridae—hawks and eagles (217 species)

    Family Pandionidae—osprey (1 species)

    Family Falconidae—falcons and caracaras
(62 species)

Order Galliformes—gallinaceous birds and allies
(4 families; 268 species)

    Family Cracidae—guans, chachalacas, and
curassows (44 species)

    Family Megapodiidae—mallee fowl and brush
turkeys (12 species)

Family Numididae—guinea fowl (7 species)

Family Phasianidae—pheasants, quails, partridges, peafowl, and chickens (205 species)

Order Gruiformes—cranes and rails (11 families; 209 species)

Family Rallidae—rails, gallinules, and coots (142 species)

Family Heliornithidae—sun-grebes or finfoots (3 species)

Family Rhynochetidae—kagu (1 species)

Family Eurypygidae—sun bittern (1 species)

Family Mesitornithidae—roatelos (mesites) (3 species)

Family Turnicidae—bustard quails (14 species)

Family Gruidae—cranes (15 species)

Family Aramidae—limpkin (1 species)

Family Psophiidae—trumpeters (3 species)

Family Cariamidae—seriemas (2 species)

Family Otididae—bustards (24 species)

Order Charadriiformes—gulls, auks, and waders (18 families; 323 species)

Family Jacanidae—jacanas (8 species)

Family Rostratulidae—painted snipe (2 species)

Family Scolopacidae—sandpipers, woodcocks, phalaropes, and turnstones (86 species)

Family Dromadidae—crab plover (1 species)

Family Chionididae—sheathbills (2 species)

Family Pluvianellidae—Magellanic Plover (1 species)

Family Pedionomidae—plains wanderer (1 species)

Family Thinocoridae—seed snipes (4 species)

Family Burhinidae—stone curlews (9 species)

Family Haematopodidae—oystercatchers (7 species)

Family Ibidorhynchidae—ibisbills (1 species)

Family Recurvirostridae—avocets and stilts (10 species)

Family Glareolidae—pratincols and coursers (16 species)

Family Charadriidae—plovers (64 species)

Family Laridae—gulls and terns (88 species)

Family Stercorariidae—skuas and jaegers (5 species)

Family Rhynchopidae—skimmers (3 species)

Family Alcidae—auks, murres, puffins (23 species)

Order Gaviiformes—loons (1 family; 5 species)

Family Gaviidae—loons (5 species)

Order Pteroclidiformes—sand grouse (1 family; 6 species)

Family Pteroclidae—sand grouse (16 species)

Order Columbiformes—pigeons and doves (1 family; 303 species)

Family Columbidae—pigeons and doves (303 species)

Order Psittaciformes—parrots (1 family; 340 species)

Family Psittacidae—parrots (268 species)

Family Cacatuidae—cockatoos (18 species)

Family Loriidae—lories (54 species)

Order Coliiformes—colies or mouse-birds (1 family; 6 species)

Family Coliidae—colies or mouse-birds (6 species)

Order Musophagiformes—turacos (1 family; 18 species)

Family Musophagidae—turacos (18 species)

Order Cuculiformes—cuckoos and roadrunners (1 family; 130 species)

Family Cuculidae—cuckoos (129 species)

Family Opisthocomidae—hoatzin (1 species)

Order Strigiformes—owls (2 families; 146 species)

Family Tytonidae—barn owls (11 species)

Family Strigidae—eagle and eared owls (135 species)

BIRD EVOLUTION

Order Caprimulgiformes—goatsuckers and nightjars
(5 families; 105 species)

 Family Steatornithidae—oilbirds (1 species)

 Family Podargidae—frogmouths (13 species)

 Family Aegothelidae—owlet frogmouths (8 species)

 Family Nyctibiidae—potoos (6 species)

 Family Caprimulgidae—true nightjars (77 species)

Order Apodiformes—swifts, hummingbirds (3 families;
428 species)

 Family Hemiprocnidae—crested swifts (4 species)

 Family Apodidae—true swifts (83 species)

 Family Trochilidae—hummingbirds (341 species)

Order Trogoniformes—trogons (1 family; 37 species)

 Family Trogonidae—trogons, quetzals (37 species)

Order Coraciiformes—rollers, kingfishers, hornbills
(10 families; 201 species)

 Family Alcedinidae—kingfishers (91 species)

 Family Todidae—toadies (5 species)

 Family Momotidae—motmots (9 species)

 Family Meropidae—bee eaters (24 species)

 Family Coraciidae—rollers (16 species)

 Family Brachypteraciidae—ground rollers
 (5 species)

 Family Leptosomatidae—cuckoo-roller (1 species)

 Family Upupidae—hoopoe (1 species)

 Family Phoeniculidae—wooded hoopoes (8 species)

 Family Bucerotidae—hornbills (45 species)

Order Piciformes—woodpeckers and toucans
(6 families; 436 species)

 Family Galbulidae—jacamars (17 species)

 Family Buconidae—puffbirds (32 species)

 Family Capitonidae—barbets (81 species)

 Family Indicatoridae—honey guides (16 species)

 Family Ramphastidae—toucans (33 species)

 Family Picidae—woodpeckers, wrynecks, and
 piculets (204 species)

Order Passeriformes—perching birds (73 families;
4,988 species)

 Suborder Tyranni—suboscines

 Family Xenicidae—New Zealand wrens (4 species)

 Family Pittidae—pittas (24 species)

 Family Eurylaimidae—broadbills (14 species)

 Family Philepittidae—asities (4 species)

 Family Dendrocolptidae—woodcreepers (52 species)

 Family Furnariidae—ovenbirds (218 species)

 Family Formicariidae—antbirds (240 species)

 Family Rhinocryptidae—tapaculos (30 species)

 Family Cotingidae—cotingas (79 species)

 Family Oxyruncidae—sharpbills (1 species)

 Family Phytotomidae—plantcutters (3 species)

 Family Pipridae—manakins (52 species)

 Family Tyrannidae—tyrant flycatchers (376 species)

 Suborder Passeres—perching birds; crow relatives

 Family Climacteridae—Australian treecreepers
 (6 species)

 Family Menuridae—Australian lyrebirds (2 species)

 Family Atrichornithidae—scrub-birds (2 species)

 Family Ptilonorhynchidae—bowerbirds (18 species)

 Family Maluridae—fairy-wrens (30 species)

 Family Acanthizidae—Australian warblers
 (75 species)

 Family Meliphagidae—Australian honey eaters
 (172 species)

 Family Callaeidae—wattlebirds (3 species)

 Family Eopsaltriidae—Australasian robins
 (34 species)

 Family Pachycephalidae—whistlers (49 species)

 Family Orthonychidae—logrunners (2 species)

 Family Pomatostomatidae—pseudo babblers
 (4 species)

Family Cinclostomatidae—quail-thrushes, whipbirds (15 species)

Family Corcoracidae—Australian Chough, Apostlebird (2 species)

Family Monarchidae—monarch flycatchers (132 species)

Family Dicruridae—drongos (20 species)

Family Corvidae—crows, jays, magpies (106 species)

Family Paradisaeidae—birds of paradise (42 species)

Family Artamidae—wood swallows (10 species)

Family Craticidae—bellmagpies (11 species)

Family Grallinidae—mudnest-builders (2 species)

Family Oriolidae—Old World orioles (25 species)

Family Campephagidae—caterpillar birds (70 species)

Family Irenidae—fairy bluebirds and leafbirds (14 species)

Family Vireonidae—vireos (43 species)

Family Laniidae—shrikes (73 species)

Family Vangidae—vangas (13 species)

Suborder Passeres—perching birds—thrush relatives

Family Bombycillidae—(8 species)

Family Dulidae—palmchat (1 species)

Family Cinclidae—dippers (5 species)

Family Turdidae—thrushes (275 species)

Family Mimidae—mockingbirds and thrashers (31 species)

Family Sturnidae—starlings (111 species)

Family Muscicapidae—Old World flycatchers (153 species)

Suborder Passeres—Old World insecteaters

Family Sittidae—nuthatches (23 species)

Family Certhiidae—typical creepers (6 species)

Family Troglodytidae—wrens (60 species)

Family Aegithalidae—long-tailed tits (7 species)

Family Hirudinidae—swallows and martins (80 species)

Family Pycnonotidae—bulbuls (123 species)

Family Zosteropidae—white-eyes (83 species)

Family Sylviidae—Old World warblers (361 species)

Family Timaliidae—babblers (257 species)

Family Rhabdornithidae—Philippine creepers (2 species)

Family Paridae—titmice (47 species)

Family Remizidae—penduline tits (10 species)

Suborder Passeres—weaver finch relatives

Family Alaudidae—larks (78 species)

Family Passeridae—Old World sparrows, rock sparrows (37 species)

Family Estrildidae—waxbills (127 species)

Family Motacillidae—wagtails and pipits (54 species)

Family Prunellidae—hedge sparrows (accentors) (12 species)

Family Ploceidae—typical weavers (107 species)

Family Promeropidae—sugarbirds (2 species)

Family Dicaeidae—flower-peckers (50 species)

Family Nectariniidae—sunbirds (117 species)

Family Fringillidae—chaffinches (122 species)

Family Drepanididae—Hawaiian honeycreepers (23 species)

Suborder Passeres—nine-primaried songbirds

Family Parulidae—American wood warblers (126 species)

Family Emberizidae—tanagers, buntings, New World sparrows, cardinals, grosbeaks, Flushcapped Finch (560 species)

Family Icteridae—American blackbirds, troupials, meadowlarks, and orioles (95 species)

FEATHERS AND FLIGHT

The feather we examined earlier in the chapter is a contour feather, one of four kinds of feathers that birds typically have. The contour feather gives shape to the bird's body, and those of the wings are specialized for flight. Every contour feather has a flat vane bisected by a central shaft. The shaft can be hollow, and the portion closest to the skin is often an enlarged quill. From a distance, the vane appears to be a single piece, but under the microscope you can see the barbs that make up the vane as well as even smaller barbules and hooks that hold the feather together. The barbules are hooked over one another in a herringbone pattern to create a surprisingly strong, yet lightweight, single structure. If barbs become unhooked, the bird can rezip them together by drawing them through its bill as it preens its feathers. As you watch birds, you will see that they spend much of their time adjusting and preening their feathers, zipping them together with their bills, and oiling them to keep them in perfect flying condition. A bird's life literally depends upon the condition of its plumage.

Other Feathers   Down feathers have no barbules and are specialized to conserve body heat. Down is typically found below contour feathers, next to a bird's skin. Through fluffing and preening, birds arrange their down feathers to create layers of dead air space that can be warmed by body heat. It is not uncommon to see birds (Great Horned Owls, for example) that incubate their eggs during snowy weather with a layer of unmelted snow on their backs—proof that body heat does not seep

A Blue Jay (Cyanocitta cristata) preens its feathers, removing dust and dirt, realigning barbs and barbules and spreading a thin film of oil.

back feather

thigh feather

right primary

head feather

tail feather

left primary

through the layer of down beneath the contour feathers.

Powder down is a specialized kind of down feather that disintegrates as it grows. As a heron, bittern, hawk, or parrot preens, its skin becomes dusted with a whitish powder from these special feathers.

Filoplume feathers are hairlike and form bristles around the mouths of swallows and goatsuckers. They also form the luxurious eyelashes of rheas, emus, and ostriches.

A fallen feather from a Steller's Jay (Cyanocitta stelleri) demonstrates its waterproof coating of oil.

Flight   Because the shaft of a flight feather is closer to its leading edge, the leading edge is wider in cross section, while the trailing edge is narrower. Because of this curvature, air above the feather has a greater distance to travel than does air below the feather. Air rushes beneath the feather, creating an area of higher pressure. As a result, the feather lifts in flight. We call this structure an airfoil. You can test this principle for yourself by holding a piece of paper between your thumbs and index fingers and allowing it to curve back over your hands. Now, blow at the curved edge of the paper and watch as it rises. You are creating a curved airfoil similar to the design of each flight as well as each wing.

We do not completely understand how birds fly, but we do know that the inner and outer portions of the wing have different functions. The inner portion with the secondary flight feathers attached acts as an airfoil to produce lift, while the outer portion with the primaries produces thrust and has a more complicated action.

If you carefully examine photos of a bird in flight, you will see that each wingbeat can be divided into a downstroke and an upstroke.

As the wings are brought down, the primary feathers are not stiff like the secondaries, but instead bend upward and twist so that they are at a steep angle to the direction in which the bird

Above: *Hummingbirds have high-speed wings that describe a figure-8 pattern and generate lift on both up- and downstroke. Here, a Broad-billed hummingbird (Cyanthus latirostris) hovers in mid-air as it feeds on a hibiscus flower (left).*

Left: *These contour feathers from the neck of a female Northern Shoveler (Anas clypeata) gives shape to the duck's body while providing a waterproof, insulating wetsuit that allows the duck to swim and dabble without losing body heat.*

Below: *In the diagram below, air passes smoothly over the bird's wing. When the bird slows by angling the wing downward, turbulence arises. The bird then raises the alula, ensuring a smooth flow of air even when flying slowly.*

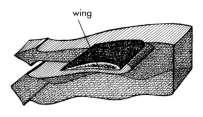
wing

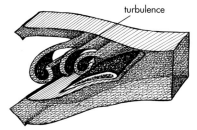
turbulence

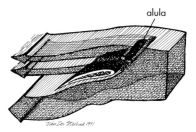
alula

is traveling. The lower surfaces of the primaries cut the air like the propeller blades of a helicopter; this action thrusts the bird forward. In essence, the bird "rows" through the air. Although most people know that on the upstroke the wings are drawn up and back, they don't readily realize that as this happens, the primary feathers twist in the opposite direction so that their upper surfaces cut through the air like minipropellers. Thus, the bird has power, lift, and thrust on both down-stroke and upstroke. This powered upstroke is especially important in birds that hover, such as hummingbirds, kingfishers, terns, and some hawks and falcons, and passerine birds that use fast,

B I R D   E V O L U T I O N

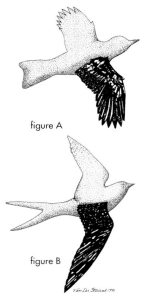

figure A

figure B

Elliptical wings (figure A) *are characteristic of birds who dart between branches and maneuver quickly in small places. High-speed wings* (figure B) *are swept back and are long and narrow with pointed tips. Soaring wings* (figure C) *are the avian equivalent of the glider. They maximize lift at the expense of maneuverability. High-lift wings* (figure D) *have wing slotting and the alula to create greater lift.*

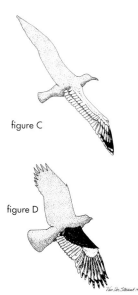

figure C

figure D

steep takeoffs rather than the slow, angled ones characteristic of waterfowl.

Kinds of Wings All wings are not alike. There are four basic wing designs, with most birds incorporating some features of each. Elliptical wings of warblers, doves, sparrows, and woodpeckers are wide and rather stubby. They are an adaptation for darting between branches and quick maneuvering in small spaces. Watch for the typical silhouette of these wings and you will see that they have "fingers" at their ends, formed as the primary feathers are held apart from one another. This "wing-slotting" accentuates the lift that each primary can generate and compensates for the small wing area of these birds.

High-speed wings of swallows, swifts, falcons, and sandpipers are moderately long and swept back with very slender, pointed tips. These birds seldom have wingtip-slotting and fly along at incredible speeds: Sandpipers fly at 109 mph (175 kph); peregrine falcons dive upon their prey at over 200 mph (320 kph)—almost too fast for the human eye to follow.

Soaring wings are long and narrow. Frigate birds, albatrosses, and gannets have the best aerodynamically designed wings adapted for energy-saving soaring and gliding, but their wings sacrifice maneuverability because they do not use wing-slotting.

High-lift wings are specialized for power when a bird is carrying a heavy load in its talons. Owls, vultures, eagles, ospreys, and hawks have wings that are even more muscular at their leading edges, creating greater lift (technically these are called cambered wings). They typically use wing-slotting and fly at steep angles because they erect a baffle at the leading edge of the wing to make air flow over it more evenly, especially during slow flight. This baffle, actually a miniature auxiliary wing formed by feathers attached to the bird's thumb, is called the alula. Watch for it, too, in birds with weak flight and slow takeoffs—turkeys, peacocks, chickens, quail, pheasants, and grouse.

Evolution of Flight

We are not sure exactly when birds began to fly, but we know that feathers and flight go back to the Late Jurassic Period, some 160 million years ago. We know that the ability to fly gave the ancestors of birds great advantages. The air was full of flying insects, a high-quality food source that is rich in protein. Flight gave escape from the many carnivorous reptiles and amphibians and allowed protobirds and birds to colonize new habitats. What is unclear at present is exactly how flight happened.

Gulls soar on ocean winds and updrafts, seeking food with minimal expenditure of energy.

Trees-Down or Ground-Up?

There are two contrasting theories of how powered, high-lift flight might have evolved. Some authorities

Above left: *The Herring Gull* (Larus argentatus) *is common on every North American coast. It is often seen soaring, taking advantage of turbulent air near the sea. Primarily scavengers, Herring Gulls can usually be found at garbage dumps and harbors, looking for discarded food.* **Above right:** *Families of Snow Geese* (Chen caerulescens) *migrate to wintering grounds, where they form huge flocks at safe roosting sites. The flocks break up to feed during the day, but reconvene at night.*

speculate that protobirds began to fly by first climbing up to high branches and then jumping off and gliding down as flying squirrels do. This is the "trees-down theory" in a nutshell. Others favor the idea that the first attempts at flight were the gliding hops of early birds that became airborne as a result of racing along the ground with wings outstretched for balance—the "ground-up theory." Good arguments support each theory, but it is clear that flight ability and feathers evolved together.

FLYING MACHINE EXTRAORDINAIRE

It is wonderful to watch birds fly. Imagine a Ruby-throated Hummingbird hovering at the lip of a trumpet creeper. For an instant the emerald satin body hangs suspended from a moving blur of wings. Then, quicker than you can grab your binoculars for a closer look, the tiny bird has zoomed away. Imagine a Northern Harrier wheeling and turning close to the windblown, winter-bleached grasses of a salt marsh. You watch as it effortlessly twists and curves, riding the wind like a kite that can think. Intently looking down, the hawk pirouettes in midair, hovers for a moment, and suddenly plunges out of sight. You wait, but grow chilled and move on before the bird rises again. Imagine a cloud of Snow Geese passing overhead, wings beating steadily. Their immaculate heads and outstretched necks quaver slightly as they are silhouetted against the sun. The flock is so close that you can hear the wind whistle with each downstroke of the black-fingered wings.

Watching birds fly is one of the chief delights of birding. Starting with a feathered lizard that could run, flap, and glide, working over the course of perhaps 200 million years, natural selection has produced many variations on the basic flying mechanism. Some birds are specially built for soaring, others for hovering, long-distance flight, maneuverability, or speed. Many birds combine these attributes; penguins can even fly underwater. Although these variations exist, flight imposes strict constraints upon the anatomy and physiology of birds. Unlike other classes or vertebrates, all birds are remarkably similar. While a birder does not need to understand how birds fly to enjoy watching them, a basic understanding of the mechanics of flight will enrich your birding.

Skeletal Design   Two major demands are made upon a bird's skeleton. It must at once be able to support the weight of the bird as it perches or walks on the ground and be light enough to allow the bird to become airborne. In addition, the skeleton must be strong enough to withstand the enormous stresses of flight. Like the early attempts at manpowered flight that ended in a mass of splinters and crumpled paper, living designs that buckle in flight are quickly eliminated by natural selection. We can observe two trends in the skeletons of birds: those that minimize weight and those that produce great strength.

Light, Strong Bones   Because flight demands that birds discard excess baggage to lighten their bodies, birds have fewer bones than humans or other vertebrates do. In some parts of the skeleton, bones have become fused together or have been reduced in size.

Skull Features   A bird has no teeth. Instead, a lightweight, horny beak takes over the manipulative function while, internally, a muscular gizzard grinds up food. A bird's skull bones are much thinner than those of a human and are fused together to make a strong, one-piece braincase. The jawbone of a bird is a delicate wisp compared to the jawbone of a human. To underscore how much lighter a bird's skull is than a mammal's: A rat's skull is 1.25 percent of its total body weight, while a pigeon's is only 0.21 percent—six times lighter.

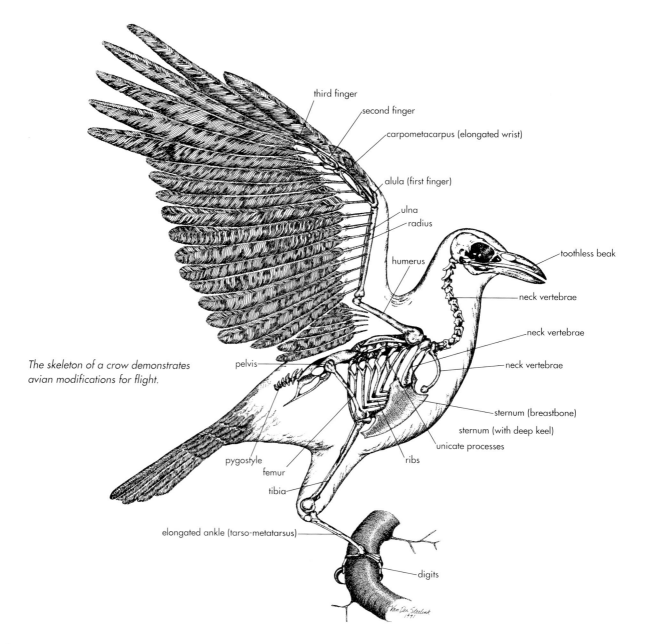

third finger

second finger

carpometacarpus (elongated wrist)

alula (first finger)

ulna

radius

humerus

toothless beak

neck vertebrae

neck vertebrae

neck vertebrae

The skeleton of a crow demonstrates avian modifications for flight.

pelvis

sternum (breastbone)

sternum (with deep keel)

unicate processes

pygostyle

femur

ribs

tibia

elongated ankle (tarso-metatarsus)

digits

Limb Bones The long limb bones of birds are hollow and contain air sacs instead of marrow. Air sacs are extensions of a bird's lungs, and technically, bones containing them are called "pneumatic." Diagonal braces strengthen hollow bones internally, much like the struts within an airplane's wing. Many bones of the bird's wrists, hands, legs, ankles, and feet are fused together, but a comparison of wing and human arm shows the same general bony plan. Birds have an unbelievably light skeleton; it is common for a bird's feathers to weigh more than its bones do. For example, the bones of a Bald Eagle weigh only 10 ounces (272 g), while its feathers weigh 25 ounces (700 g).

Keeled Breastbone In the discussion of *Archaeopteryx*, I mentioned that paleontologists speculate that it was a weak flier because it had no keel on its breastbone. Flying birds (as compared with flightless rails, rheas, kiwis, and ostriches) have a deep, bony projection on the breastbone that anchors massive wing muscles.

The backbone has areas that are fused together, making it rigid and strong, rather than flexible. The ribs have overlapping bony flaps that also give rigidity and strength to the body. The wishbone and a second bone, the coracoid, form a pair of strong struts that brace the breastbone and give support at the wing joint. All these features allow the bird's backbone, ribs, breastbone, and hip and shoulder girdles to form a lightweight, rigid-yet-strong, bony box to which the neck bones and the ball-and-socket joints of the wings and the hips attach. The relative rigidity of a bird's torso is compensated for by the mobility of its numerous neck vertebrae. Unlike mammals, which generally have only seven neck bones, birds have between eight and twenty-four, depending upon the species. These are moved by an extraordinarily complex set of long, stringy muscles. In many respects, the flexibility of a bird's neck resembles that of a snake's body. Although birds cannot

Great Egret (Casmerodius albus) *in flight.*

bend from the waist to touch their toes, they can reach down with their long, flexible necks and easily peck at objects on the ground. They also can reach behind to preen their tail feathers, and that snaky neck allows them to smear oil from the gland above their tails onto their crown feathers. Any forward bending, though, comes mostly from the hip joint.

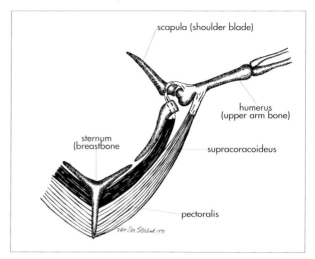

Breast muscles attach to both sternum and humerus. The pectoralis muscle provides power for the downstroke of flight, while contraction of the supracoracoideus, located beneath the pectoralis, pulls the humerus back on the upstroke.

Muscle Power   Anyone who has ever eaten chicken knows that bird muscles are not equally distributed. Backs, shanks, feet, and wings have little meat; most flesh is found in the breast and the portions of the wings and legs that are closest to the body. Instead of having large muscles on their wings or on their lower legs as humans do, birds have concentrated their muscles near the body and move the distant parts (for example, the feet and toes) with long, slender tendons. The placement of muscles is a specialization for flight that lowers the bird's center of gravity. It improves balance and gives additional power in flight.

Wing Muscles   An understanding of how wing muscles move a bird's skeleton, providing the power for flight, gives an extra dimension to birdwatching. Only two muscles are involved; one large, the other smaller. Both are called flight muscles. The larger flight muscle (pectoralis) pulls the wing down, and the smaller flight muscle (supracoracoideus) raises it. The larger muscle is familiar to anyone who has ever eaten chicken breast; the smaller one lies beneath it and can only be seen by moving the larger muscle aside. Both are anchored to the keel of the breastbone, as well as to the wishbone and the coracoid.

The location of the smaller flight muscle is another unique feature of bird anatomy, one that is associated with flight. In humans the equivalent muscle—one that draws the upper arm back toward

The powerful wings of the Trumpeter Swan (Olor buccinator) are used for display and defense, as well as flight. Destruction of breeding grounds for agriculture pushed the species near extinction in the 1930s; recovery efforts are now under way.

the spine—is located on the back, connected to the shoulder blade (scapula). You can test this for yourself by holding your arm out straight and to one side, parallel to the floor. Now, draw your arm back toward your spine. You will feel muscles working in your back. If you were a bird, these muscles would be in your breast, giving you a lower center of gravity and better balance in flight.

From its anchor on the breastbone, wishbone, and coracoid, the large flight muscle attaches to the underside of the upper arm bone. It is easy to see how a contraction of this muscle will pull down on the upper arm bone and the wing that is formed by the bird's lower arm, wrist, and finger bones. The action of the smaller muscle is more complicated. A long tendon extends from the end of this muscle. It loops over the shoulder blade and attaches to the upper surface of the upper arm bone, forming a pulleylike mechanism. When it shortens, this smaller muscle pulls on the tendon and lifts the wing, making an upstroke. Why is one flight muscle so much larger than the

The male Painted Bunting (Passerina ciris), found in the eastern United States, is one of the most colorful birds in North America. When a male sings, he perches in the open; more often, the birds are found in thickets and are hard to spot.

other? Probably because it can afford to be. Flight power comes from the downstroke; birds can often let the rush of air lift their wings and thus save muscular energy.

"Red" vs. "White" Muscles   Everyone recognizes that chickens have two kinds of meat, dark and light. These translate into "red" and "white" muscles, which differ in their capacity for long, sustained contractions, as well as in their speed of contraction. "Red" muscles are red because they contain myoglobin, a molecule that provides extra oxygen needed for muscle contraction. "White" muscles have less myoglobin.

Because myoglobin gives red muscles extra oxygen, they are good at long, sustained contractions, such as those in the flight muscles of birds steadily flying on long-distance migrations. On the other hand, "white" muscles are better at extremely rapid, short-lasting bursts of activity. With this information, you should be able to determine why ducks have all dark meat (all red muscles) and why chickens have white breast meat and dark leg meat. What color muscles would quail have? What about hummingbirds?

Bird Breathing   A mammal breathes as the movement of its diaphragm (a sheet of muscle that separates the chest from the abdominal cavity) and chest ventilate a set of passive lungs.

In mammals, air moves in and out like the tide, and oxygen and carbon dioxide are exchanged in alveoli, the tiny, thin-walled sacs of the lungs. Birds have a radically different plan in which air moves through the lungs in only one direction; there is no diaphragm. Instead, movements of the breastbone and ribs increase and decrease body volume. Although a bird's lungs are not distensible, they have a breathing mechanism—six to nine air sacs connected to the lungs. These air sacs expand and contract with the movements of the surrounding muscles, especially in flight. The air sacs act like bellows to propel air out through this one-way system.

Air is inhaled through the nostrils or mouth. Bird lungs are as porous to air as a sponge is to water, and most of the air bypasses the lungs and goes to the rear sets of air sacs. From the rear air sacs, the air travels to the parabronchi of the lungs where oxygen and carbon dioxide are exchanged. Parabronchi are systems of parallel, thin-walled tubules surrounded by capillaries. The air then moves to the front sets of air sacs, another distensible bellows; these propel the air through the bronchi and tracheae to the environment.

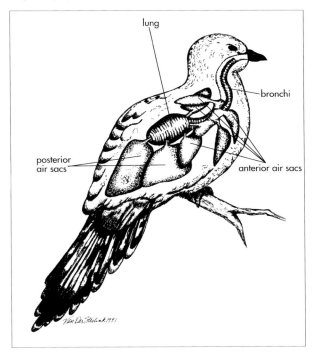

Paired air sacs extend from the lungs. The path of air is as follows: During inhalation air goes through the lungs to the posterior air sacs. It then passes to the parabronchi (not shown) where oxygen and carbon dioxide are exchanged. Air then moves to the anterior air sacs, into the bronchi and tracheae, and out the mouth or nostrils. In all of this the air sacs act like bellows to move the air through all of the passages of the respiratory system.

Hyperefficient Breathing   The muscles, brain, and senses of a flying bird must have a steady and abundant supply of energy, or the bird will crash and probably die. Sugar in the form of glucose is the source for energy within any animal's body. Oxygen is needed to break down sugar and release its stored energy, thus fueling the molecular mechanisms of muscle contraction and nerve conduction. Because of their one-way breathing system, which extracts oxygen twice from a lungful of air, birds are much more efficient than mammals at wringing oxygen from the air they breathe: Birds can extract 31 percent of the oxygen in air, while mammals can only extract 24 percent. This greater efficiency allows birds to fly at altitudes as great as 3.6 miles or 6,000 meters—where human fliers must wear oxygen masks.

The efficiency of the one-way, air sac breathing plan is supplemented by the incredible rate at which it functions. There is a general correlation between speed of breathing and a bird's size: Chickens ventilate twenty times per minute, pigeons twenty-six times per minute, starlings eighty-four times per minute, and hummingbirds an incredible 330 times per minute.

The Canada Goose (Branta canadensis) is widely distributed in North America. Flocks are made up of family groups, which remain together through fall and spring migration, until the young are a year old.

CHAPTER 2

Bird Life

"Which came first, the chicken or the egg?"

*I*magine an endless line of hens, chicks, and eggs stretching backward in time: Hen Z grew from Egg Z, laid by Hen Y, who grew from Egg Y, laid by Hen X, the product of Egg X, laid by Hen W...Naming hens with letters from known and unknown alphabets, the line spirals back perhaps 200 million years, until we finally reach the egg that hatched into Hen Alpha, the very first bird. We look around to find the parent of Egg Alpha, and see a feathered reptile, perched on a nearby branch, preening its breast feathers. Then the answer to the vexing riddle becomes clear. The egg came first. Birds inherited the habit of egg laying from their reptilian ancestors and have retained it because egg laying is strangely suited to flight.

The reproductive tracts of the bird are drastically modified to reduce weight. While all male reptiles (except the tuatara from New Zealand) have some kind of copulatory organ to ensure that sperm are safely passed from male to female, only a few kinds of male birds have a copulatory organ. Ratite birds such as tinamous, ostriches, and curassows, as well as carinale birds such as storks, flamingos, ducks, geese, chickens, and their galliform relatives have penises, but all other groups of birds are have-nots: They lack a male copulatory organ. Instead, after appropriate courtship, the male bird balances himself on

The cloacal kiss

the middle of the female's back and, with considerable help from her, brings his cloaca into contact with hers, squirting sperm into her reproductive tract in a "cloacal kiss." Excess baggage is similarly reduced in female birds, which develop only a single ovary and oviduct.

To further reduce weight, the sex organs of both male and female are active, and thus heavy, for only a part of the year; they atrophy and become nearly invisible once the breeding season is over. In males, depending upon the species, testes have a 200 to 300 percent weight gain as the breeding season approaches; in females the increase is even more spectacular: Ovaries and their associated egg-producing tubes can swell to 1,500 percent of their shrunken weight. This seasonal weight gain of reproductive organs is also typical of reptiles. Birds have retained and modified this reptilian trait because it fits well with their fast-paced, high-energy-consuming metabolism.

THE INCREDIBLE EGG

Birds are the only class of vertebrates with no species that bears live young. While fishes, frogs, and toads, snakes, and mammals have species with live-born young, all birds lay eggs. As you may have guessed, this is another adaptation for reducing weight to make flight less energy-consuming. Furthermore, each egg is extruded from the female's body and deposited into a nest quite soon after it is completely formed within her oviduct. Unlike fish, amphibians, and reptiles, which internally accumulate an entire clutch of eggs and lay them all at one time, birds lay single eggs at intervals as short as a day (chickens, ducks, geese, and most passerines) or as long as four to eight days (megapodes or mounted birds).

The egg provides shelter and food for the developing chick. Although it may seem to be a lifeless object, an egg is metabolically active. It breathes. Oxygen, water vapor, and carbon dioxide pass through the porous shell. Not all eggs are egg-shaped. Owls lay nearly spherical eggs, and the eggs of auks, guillemots, and other cliff-nesters are shaped like tops so that they don't roll off ledges but instead roll in a safer, semicircular path. Eggshells differ in thickness. The African Francolins are heavy-footed partridgelike birds, and it is said that the shells of their eggs are so thick that you can practically bounce them off a wall. At the opposite extreme are the soft, nearly transparent eggshells of the Indian Woodpecker, which lays eggs in the nest it digs in woody ant mounds.

DDT and Eggshell-Thinning
When an animal like a fish or rabbit eats food that is contaminated with DDT, the pesticide is not eliminated, but instead stored within its body, usually within the fat deposits. When a predator subsequently eats this DDT-contaminated prey, it receives all of the fat-stored DDT, too. If the predator is an osprey, Peregrine Falcon, or one of the many species of eagle, the large dosage of DDT that it gets along with each normal meal

Top: *The precocial young of the Black Oystercatcher* (Haematopus bachmani) *are able to fly about 35 days after hatching, but they will be dependent upon their parents for several months as they master the technique of opening mussels, clams, and other shellfish.*

Above: *Kildeer* (Charadrius vociferous) *nests are so well-camouflaged that they are almost impossible to spot.*

will accumulate and eventually affect the raptor's metabolism of calcium. This altered state shows itself in eggs with shells that are too poor in calcium to support the weight of the brooding parent. These fragile eggs are crushed, and the entire

One of the first signs that pesticides threatened birds was die-offs of American Robins (Turdus migratorius) in the 1950s. Earthworms, a dietary staple for this species, accumulated the toxins, poisoning the birds that ate them.

clutch must be replaced, usually with a second set of DDT-thinned shells that suffer the same fate. As you can imagine, bird species susceptible to DDT-thinned eggshells cannot maintain their normal population numbers. Ospreys, Peregrine Falcons, and eagles of all kinds suffer from eggshell-thinning wherever DDT is sprayed to kill insects. Only heroic human efforts have saved these birds from extinction. Although the use of DDT is now illegal in the Unites States, Canada, Britain, and Australia, manufacturers are still sending tons of it to other countries, notably in South America and Asia. Bird populations will continue to decline from eggshell-thinning as long as DDT is used.

Normally, the eggshell serves as a reservoir of calcium that is drawn upon by the developing embryo. As a result, the shell naturally becomes thinner as incubation proceeds and the embryo incorporates the calcium into its growing body.

Eggshell Colors   We usually think of eggs as being immaculate and white, but bird eggs come in many colors, some of them protective. Although most species have an egg with a recognizable size, shape, color, and pattern, so that the egg of a wren is distinguishable from that of a starling, for example, some species can lay eggs of many colors. The Common Murre lays a rainbow of eggs, though not necessarily in the same nest. Murre eggs can be deep blue-green, reddish, yellow-red, pale blue, beige, or white. They can be marked with bright red, brown, or black lines, squiggles, blotches, or spots, or they can be unicolored. Brood parasites (birds that do not nest themselves, but lay their eggs in the nests of other species) such as the European Cuckoo can produce eggs to match those of the species they are victimizing.

"It's a Yolk, Son!"   We normally think of an egg as having two portions, white and yolk, but a closer examination shows that the structure of an egg is much more complicated. If you have ever noticed a faint, white spot on the yellow yolk of a hen's egg, you have seen the germinal spot: the place in the yolk where the embryo rests. Yolk supplies food to the embryo, and although we normally consider it a mere mass of yellow goo, it actually has a concentric structure made of alternating layers of brighter and paler yellow yolk. The yolk is stabilized within the white of the egg by the layered structure of the albumen and by thick ropes of albumen, called chalazae, that support the yolk within the white.

Human interference in the environment is the greatest danger faced by this nesting Bald Eagle (Haliaeetus leucocephalus).

A parent bird usually incubates the eggs by squatting over them and pressing its brood patches against them. Brood patches are paired areas of bare skin on the breast that are warmer than other parts of the bird's body because of a rich network of blood vessels. About three times a day the parent reaches down and turns the egg with its beak. As an egg is turned the yolk rotates within a thin layer of albumen so that the germinal spot is always closest to the parent's warm skin. The chalazae hold the yolk in place as it freely rotates.

HATCHING

Soon before hatching the chick begins to cheep within its eggshell, perhaps signaling its parents and the other chicks in the clutch that it is ready to emerge. This is a behavior also seen in eggs and hatchlings of alligators and crocodiles and may indicate the common ancestry of birds and reptiles. Like hatchling reptiles, chicks have an egg tooth on the tip of their beaks: a hard deposit of calcium that they use to hammer their way out of the eggshell.

Above Left: *Why are the eggs of so many birds colored in heavenly shades of blue? The exuberance of nature? An accident? No one knows for sure, but the eggs of the Western Bluebird* (Sialia mexicana) *are one example of this lovely mystery.*

Above Right: *These Black Oystercatcher* (Haematopus bachmani) *eggs have cryptic coloration that protects them from egg predators such as ravens.*

Bird species have young that are either naked and helpless at birth ("altricial," based on the Latin word for "nurse") or young that hatch out covered with down and are able to follow their parents and feed themselves only hours after hatching ("precocial"). One extreme in precocial birds is the pheasant, which can fly a mere three days after it has hatched. In altricial species, on the other hand, it can take weeks for the chicks to be able to do more than beg for food, eat, jostle their nestmates, and sleep. Finches and warblers fledge in only eight days, while swifts take three to six weeks and albatrosses take six months from hatching to first flight. Altricial hatchlings are practically cold-blooded. Unable to maintain the normal bird body temperature of 106° F (41.1° C), they must be brooded by a parent if they are to survive.

Care of Precocial Young   Precocial species like plovers and ducks protect their young by trying to distract a predator with a display in which the parent bird pretends to be injured. This display, often accompanied by loud cries, leads the predator away from the eggs or young. When these are out of danger, the parent flies away. The cryptic appearance of most down-covered precocial young is excellent camouflage. It is especially effective when coupled with the instinct of many precocial chicks to remain still when they are in danger. Precocial species show their young how to peck and teach them, by example, what is edible. Many adult birds with precocial youngsters will fight to protect their flock of young.

Care of Altricial Young   In the days and perhaps weeks that a nestling is growing, the parent birds are in constant attendance. Males give up territorial defense to help the female feed and brood the helpless young. The kind of food and how frequently it arrives at the nest both vary with species. Baby Storm Petrels are fed a single huge meal once or twice a week, while passerine parents may return more than twenty times per hour with beaks full of insects or crops full of seeds and fruit. This intense activity takes a toll on the parent birds, and female songbirds may lose 10 to 20 percent of their body weight while dashing about feeding their incessantly begging nestlings. Some nestlings feed only of food dangled from the parent's bill, while others reach into the parent's crop. A few, such as hawks, feed themselves from food left at the nest site by their parents. The sight of the colorful, gaping maw of a begging baby bird seems to stimulate an automatic feeding reaction in songbirds. Herring Gull chicks peck at the red spot on their parent's bill, causing regurgitation of food, and kingfishers, which nest in dim, earthen tunnels, have a similar regurgitation spot, but it is white.

Within the shell an egg has chalazae that stabilize the egg yolk. The embryo develops from the germinal disk. After using their beaks to puncture the egg membrane, chicks hammer their way out of the egg. A hard deposit of calcium on their bill, the egg tooth, and a well-developed muscle, at the back of the skull, called the "hatching muscle," both help them to escape from the confines of the egg.

You can learn a great deal about birds by watching their activities at the nest. If you are fortunate enough to have birds nesting in your backyard, you will be able to watch without disturbing them. Many birds will desert a nest if a predator (such as you) distresses them, so try to be as secretive as possible and don't get too close to the nest or the parents. Your patience will be rewarded by the sight of healthy fledglings teetering in the branches of your lilac tree. Do parents share equally in tasks of incubating, brooding, and feeding the young? How often does a parent return with food? How many chicks are in the nest? Learn to recognize the "change of shift" call that many songbirds give when one parent relieves the other. Keep records of your observations and add to them from year to year.

Even after the nestlings have grown feathers and deserted the nest, many continue to beg for handouts from their parents. In midsummer you can see gangs of burly, adolescent robins, sparrows, or Blue Jays that follow parent birds and gape, fluff their feathers, and shiver their wings like nestlings begging (sometimes demanding, it seems) to be fed. By contrast, in some other species, such as the Moorhen and House Martin, the young may help the adults to raise subsequent broods. Unmated adult Mexican Jays function as nest assistants.

After fledging, the immature birds feed, perfect their powers of flight, and fatten through the summer months. Depending upon the species, fledglings may form a small flock with others of their age or stay with their parents in a family group that forages cooperatively through the winter. Parents may raise a second or third brood, or, as with Mourning Doves, attempt five clutches of eggs per summer, if food is abundant.

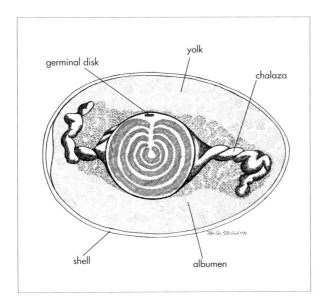

"Feed me! Feed me!" demand these begging baby American robins. The yellow rims of their beaks make an eye-catching target for a harried parent bird with a beakful of wriggling worms.

MIGRATION: DANGEROUS PASSAGE

Migrants are birds that move from summer breeding grounds to winter feeding grounds, while residents are species that stay in one locality all year. Migration has many advantages. It allows birds to escape severe weather, reach a plentiful food supply for both themselves and their broods of ever-hungry chicks, gain additional space for territory and nesting, and elude predators and parasites. Migration is also dangerous and metabolically draining. Birds that migrate from Europe to Southern Africa typically lose between 26 and 44 percent of their body weight while crossing the Sahara Desert. Those that cross the North Sea going from the British Isles to Continental Europe typically lose 20 percent of their body weight. In addition, a bird must somehow know when to migrate so that it arrives at the breeding grounds at the proper time; it must know where to go and how to get there. It must not get lost, but if it does get lost, it must have some internal map to help it reach others of its species. The migrator must have enough energy in the form of fat reserves for the journey, it must elude predators en route, and it must be able to recognize its breeding ground once it has arrived. Although ornithologists know much more about migration than they did thirty years ago, no one completely understands how birds migrate. Keep this in mind the next time you see a high-flying skein of geese overhead, honking as they head south.

A flock of Western Sandpipers (Calidris mawi) *during spring migration.*

Environmental Clues

As days grow longer from late winter to early spring, the greater amount of natural light stimulates hormonal changes in birds belonging to species that are genetically predisposed to migrate. For birds wintering in equatorial regions, where day length does not vary, there are fewer good explanations for the stimuli that sends birds northward to breed. Population explosions of insects, environmental scents, amount of rainfall, and low-frequency sounds generated by jet streams, ocean waves, and winds have all been suggested as possible environmental cues.

The hypothalamus, a pea-sized gland situated at the base of the bird's brain, influences the nearby anterior pituitary gland to release hormones that will cause a bird's nearby invisible internal sex organs to increase in size. As the days lengthen, (or shorten, in the case of Australian Lyrebirds and Emperor Penguins), the gonads (ovaries and testes) begin to produce sex hormones that further alter the bird's metabolism and behavior.

Fuel for Long-Distance Fliers   Birds accumulate fat reserves that provide the fuel for migratory journeys. In small birds fat normally makes up only three to ten percent of the body weight, but just prior to migration the fat reserve increases to 40 percent or even 50 percent of body weight. Hormones also change bird behavior. The birds begin to form flocks, grow increasingly nervous, and start to practice the songs that are part of courtship behavior. In the male bird, newly developed sperm are stored in the cloaca and produce a swelling that has a function similar to the sperm-cooling scrotal sac of male mammals.

Even though we are certain that light-influenced hormones prepare the mind and body of a bird for migration, no one knows exactly how increased day length influences either the pineal gland or the hypothalamus.

Snow Geese (Chen caerulescens) *winter at the Bosque National Wildlife Refuge in New Mexico, along with Canada Geese, Sandhill Cranes, and other waterfowl. Watching the flocks take off at dawn to feed is a popular activity for local and visiting birders.*

Where Do They Go?   Of the roughly 4,000 species of birds that migrate, most move north in summer and south in winter. The map on page 51 shows the major worldwide migration routes. Notice that, although there are some east-to-west routes, mainly where east-west mountain ranges intervene, most migrations involve north-to-south movements. Breeding in northern latitudes allows parent birds to raise more as well as larger and stronger chicks. This is because there is abundant food (especially insects) and ample time to hunt for food in the much longer northern spring and summer days. (Days are always twelve hours long in the tropics.)

Migration Examples

Species	Distance	Time	Breeding Ground	Wintering Ground
Arctic Tern	10,800 miles (18,000 km)	114+ days	Arctic Circle	Antarctic shores
Bobolink	6,750 miles (11,250 km)	not known	Northern United States	Argentina
Bristle-Thighed Curlew	6,000 miles (10,000 km)	not known	Alaska	Polynesia
Hudsonian Godwit	2,880 miles (4,800 km)	30 days	Hudson, James Bays, Canada	Southern Chile and Argentina
Blackpoll Warbler	2,820 miles (4,700 km)	115 hours nonstop	New England	Lesser Antilles and Venezuela
Ruddy Turnstone	2,800 miles (4,655 km)	4 days	Alaska	Hawaii
Snow Goose	1,620 miles (2,700 km)	60 hours	James Bay, Canada	Louisiana
Blue Grouse	180 miles	minutes	winter—mountains of Idaho spring—330 yards, or 300 meters lower summer—still lower to valleys	

There are also fewer predators and fewer parasites in the north. On the tundra, parent birds can (and do) feed their young for as many as 21 hours of the 24-hour day. Making the reverse migration, moving south, allows songbirds to escape the harsh, northern winter and find food in tropical climates.

The champion long-distance migrator is the Arctic Tern, which travels 11,200 miles (18,000 km) per migration, for a total of 22,400 miles (36,000 km) per year. The Arctic Tern breeds north of the Arctic Circle in the summer of the northern hemisphere and travels to Antarctica to feed on the rich waters off the pack ice there in the southern "summer."

Migratory journeys are as varied as the more than 4,000 species that make them. Some birds make a single, nonstop flight of a few days, while others pause to refuel along the way, taking a month or so for migration. Small birds tend to feed by day and migrate at night, while larger birds with greater fat reserves tend to migrate by day and rest at night. Some insectivorous birds, like swifts and swallows, feed while they migrate.

Some species migrate in huge flocks of hundreds of thousands of birds; others have straggling migrations in small flocks. Within a single species, such as the Barn Owl, there many be a population that migrates (in the northern United States, for example) and a sedentary population that does not (in the southern United States, for example). In species like the Song Sparrow, migration is not a hard and fixed rule. Within a single population, some birds migrate and some do not. Migratory journeys can be globe-spanning, as in the Arctic Tern species, or merely up and down a mountainside, as in the Pine Grosbeak of the Rocky Mountains.

Why Don't They Get Lost?   One of the mysteries of migration is that long, migratory journeys are often taken by immature birds or first-season adults returning to the breeding

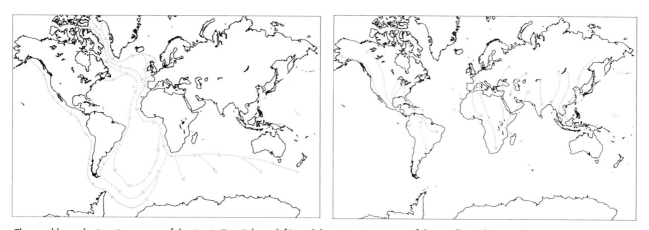

The southbound migration routes of the Arctic Tern (above left) and the migration routes of the swallow (above right).

grounds where they hatched. How do they know where to go? How do they know how to get there? How do they find their way in the dark? The problem is made even more mysterious by the fact that not only can many birds find the general geographical area where they breed, but often they return to the same exact spot year after year. Studies with penguins have shown that they are incredibly faithful to their nest sites. First-season adult male penguins typically return to a place not far from where they, themselves, were hatched. Although some scientists have hypothesized that the sense of smell may guide a penguin, much the same way that it guides breeding salmon upriver to the streams where they hatched, no on know how penguins find their way to the "old homestead." Obviously, birds have homing senses that we can only imagine, as well as built-in navigational abilities that allow them to steer a course for thousands of miles or kilometers in the dark. Natural selection continuously hones the navigational abilities of migratory birds. Those that wander off course tend to die or fail to breed successfully. Thus, they are eliminated from the population and prevented from passing their "bad genes" to the next generation of migrators.

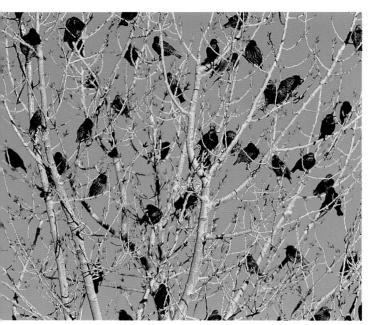

Mixed flocks of migrating blackbirds are a common sight in spring and autumn.

Ingenious experimenters have shown that birds can navigate by using the sun by day and the stars by night. It has also been found that deposits of magnetite in the neck muscles of birds may allow their head regions to function as magnetic compasses, helping to orient them in the air. This would be especially useful on cloudy or foggy nights when there are no stars to steer by. Flocking behavior also helps birds find their way; no doubt younger birds capitalize on the knowledge of older, experienced birds. Flocks are typically quite vocal in flight, cheeping and twittering as they migrate. These sounds may help maintain bird-to-bird contact within a flock, keeping the flock together and preventing midair collisions as the birds fly through the night.

Birds tend to migrate on clear rather than cloudy days. The heights at which they fly tend to be higher over water than over land and higher at night than during the day. Large birds like storks, herons, ducks, geese, swans, hawks, and eagles tend to migrate during the day when thermal air currents are generated by the sun. Birds that soar on thermals during migrations save much metabolic energy, expending only one-third as much as birds that use flapping flight.

Migration Watching   If you keep daily lists of bird species observed during migration, you will be able to accumulate personal records of the times at which various species migrate through your area in spring and in fall. Comparing your lists from year to year as well as matching your informal lists with those of other birders will give you a mental picture of how migration proceeds in

Young Canada Geese (Branta canadensis) *leave the nest within twenty-four hours of hatching, attended by both parents and already able to swim, dive, and feed. Orphaned or lost goslings may be accepted by other parents, sometimes creating large*

your region. But no matter how mentally prepared you are, you will still be swept away by the excitement of a "wave day" when otherwise birdless branches are loaded with songbirds that suddenly have appeared overnight. No matter how many times you experience bird migration, the magic remains.

COURTSHIP AND MATING

Most of us are familiar with the courtship pattern that is typical for songbirds. A territorial male sings to attract a female. They mate, build a nest, incubate the eggs she lays, and cooperatively feed and foster their growing brood. Without doubt, courtship, mating, and rearing young are the most biologically significant events in the lives of birds. And, although it should not surprise us that all bird species do not conform to this familiar pattern, the array of courtship patterns is a fascinating biological Chinese puzzle.

Imprinting on the Proper Stranger   Within the first hours after a chick hatches, an extremely rapid form of learning takes place in which the young bird associates itself with whatever large, moving object it sees. After this "critical" or "sensitive" period, the chick will follow this object; once it has grown to adulthood, it will attempt to mate with something similar to that first moving image it imprinted upon.

Imprinting is irreversible. It works quite well as a way for birds to learn to recognize a member of their own species, mainly because a parent is usually the first moving object a hatchling sees. However, things get confused when humans or farm machinery intervene. There are many hilarious stories of misimprinted goslings, chickens, and ducks following humans around as well as one hapless Ruffed Grouse who imprinted on a tractor. The misguided grouse followed its tractor about the fields, and, when the bird was sexually mature, it displayed to the tractor, not just once, but four seasons in a row.

Not all birds imprint, but many with precocial young, as well as owls, ravens, doves, and finches, use this form of species recognition. Captive raptor chicks such as condors, hawks, and falcons being raised for eventual release in the wild are fed by "puppet parents" so that they will not imprint upon humans and spoil their chances for successful future matings.

Vocal Courtship   Although great whales shriek, elephants trumpet, cats purr, dogs howl, tortoises moan, snakes hiss, frogs croak, toads trill, and fishes burp, only birds sing. And, though both sexes sing in species

Many songbirds learn species-specific song in the nest by listening to their parents. Northern Mockingbirds (Mimus polyglottos) create their song later by imitating other species. One mocker's song included over fifty different bird songs, plus a barking dog and the noise of machinery.

such as the Northern Cardinal, song usually advertises the presence of a sexually active male bird that is defending his territory and/or seeking a mate. Species that have identical-looking males and females often are the best singers. There is little sexual dimorphism (external differences between the sexes) in European Nightingales; North American Mockingbirds; Wood, Song, and Hermit Thrushes; and Veery.

Many birds sing from a perch, but there are a number of variations on this theme. Some sing while hidden from view; others sing from the ground or a low perch. Some sing only in the daytime; others, like owls, poor-wills, and their relatives, sing only at night. Some, like plovers, skylarks, and woodcocks, sing while flying. Still others, like petrels, sing in underground burrows.

Species Specific Although the novice may be familiar with only a few calls and songs, experienced birders will be able to identify hundreds of species by their vocalizations alone. Walking through the spring woods with

Birders seeking the Great Horned Owl (Bubo virginianus) sometimes go out at night. A good imitation of the owl's hooting calls will often stimulate local owls to call back.

a birdsong expert is a humbling experience. You hear a nondescript cheep or a short trill and the expert identifies the bird. The expert hears things that you don't. After a while, especially when the birds are shy and difficult to see, you may begin to think that the expert is pulling your leg.

Bird song is stereotypic and species specific. Although some birds, like the Brown Thrasher and other mimic-thrushers, incorporate the songs of other species into their own repertoires, songs and calls are a tremendous help to a birder. But beginning and intermediate birders usually don't know where to begin. With so many songs, how can they educate their ears?

Learn Bird Calls   The quickest way I know to become a better birder is to learn to listen. When you are in the field, pause often and concentrate only on listening. We civilized humans usually "tune out" most of the noises around us. As a birder, you have to reverse this tendency and "tune in" to bird vocalizations. Once you hear a bird, try to find it. Once you have located and identified it, listen carefully to the song. Can you think of a mental hook that will help you remember it? The most usual hooks are words. The White-throated Sparrow is often said to sing, "Poor Sam Peabody. Peabody, Peabody, Peabody." Your field guide will give a description of the song of each species. Do you agree or disagree with this description? Bird song is difficult to remember and notes will help. In the example from my field notes (see page 79), I mentioned that the White-throated Sparrow made a sound like the squeaker in a rubber toy. Field guides describe this sound as "a whistled whee whee whew" (Peterson), "2 or 3 short whistles, the last one lower pitched" (Robbins, et al.). For me, the sound of a squeaky toy better describes this call.

Once you become more conscious of sounds, you will be astonished at all the bird songs and calls that you never heard before. Keep in mind that recognition of a bird call by a reliable birder "counts" as much as having seen the bird.

Study   I have found that the easiest, most entertaining way to learn bird calls is to buy a specialized cassette tape or compact disc and listen to it incessantly. The commute to work, exercise time, mundane housework, can all become listening time. My current favorite is *Birding by Ear* by Walton and Lawson because, unlike other recorders of bird songs who merely roll off species after ear-deadening species, these authors highlight the differences and similarities between songs and calls. They give special attention to the tricky songs and teach lots of mental hooks that will help you remember bird vocalizations. A different, but nonetheless useful, approach is the series of audiocards marketed as *Audible Audubon*. Each card has a recording of a single species that is inserted into a miniature phonograph. It is easier to locate and learn the call of a particular species with this device, but the variety of species presented is somewhat limited. Also, the cards are fragile and the quality of recordings is sometimes uneven.

Don't expect to become an expert in bird song in a single session. Although with diligent effort you can master hundreds of songs, it will take many years of fieldwork to learn even the variations of song given by the common summer residents. But it is an interesting, challenging aspect of birding.

Shades of Monogamy   The typical songbird lifestyle is a monogamous relationship that involves one sexual partner for each individual during a particular nesting cycle. But, just like humans, birds have a spectrum of monogamy that ranges from life-long to short-lived matings. Unlike humans, who belong to a single species, the strength of the pair bond is characteristic for each bird species and probably genetically determined. Swans, geese, some species of crows, and ravens, plus Common Terns, Wrentits, Brown Creepers, White-breasted Nuthatches, and Pygmy Nuthatches are all reported to form lifetime pair bonds. Interestingly, all these species have little sexual dimorphism. A less strong bond is seen in species that remain together only until after the young have been raised. Barn Swallows, Catbirds, House Wrens, and Eastern Bluebirds follow this pattern. Or members of a pair may remate in successive breeding seasons; or they may switch part-

ners for a second brood. In ducks, pair bonds are only seasonal. Duck and drake associate closely from late winter until incubation begins, and then the drake separates from the nesting duck. Pairs of Ruby-throated Hummingbirds stay together only a few days; they separate once incubation starts. The most fleeting pair bonds are in polygamous species where the pairs remain together only during the period of copulation.

Long-lived species, like these Sandhill Cranes (Grus canadensis), may have the same mate throughout their reproductive lifetime. Birds that lose mates will usually re-pair. Members of pairs unsuccessful at breeding may split up and find new mates.

Polygamy and Promiscuity   Polygamous species may have many sexual partners in one breeding season. In polygynous species, one male will mate with several females. Ornamental plumes, plumage displays, and highly accentuated sexual dimorphism are characteristic of polygynous species such as ostriches, pheasants, grouse, and birds of paradise. In polyandrous species such as tinamous and spotted sandpipers, a single female will mate with many males, depositing eggs in nests that the males incubate. In promiscuous species, such as the Boat-tailed Grackle, copulation is indiscriminate with no formation of a pair bond at all.

Mating Rituals   In species in which the sexes look alike, ritualistic postures of mutual courtship and elaborate plumage displays prepare a female for egg production as well as synchronize the readiness of partners to successfully mate. Visual stimuli produce physiological changes in male and female. For example, in pigeons the sight of a displaying male causes the female to ovulate, and the sight of the incubating female causes the male's crop to begin to secrete pigeon's milk, the food for the nestlings.

The synchronous dancing rituals of many species of cranes, in which mates bounce up and down, leap into the air with trailing, long legs and flapping wings, stretch and jerk their necks about, and utter sharp, unearthly cries, are particularly dramatic primal ballets. The ritual dance of swans, in which floating birds face one another, necks curved, wings half-spread, and then repeatedly rear up out of the water, necks still arched, wings opened even more, is another example of mutual display. Many species of waterfowl (ducks, geese, swans,

The mating behavior of Sandhill Cranes (Grus canadensis) includes postures and jumps often called "dancing." Courtship behavior begins while birds are still in winter flocks, with young birds looking for mates and established pairs renewing their bonds.

coots, and grebes) perform water shows that typically feature "motorboating" in which displaying mates or males shoot across the water in a shower of spray. Herons and their relatives typically have mutual displays that involve synchronous head bobbing and neck stretching. While some egrets and herons have specialized breeding plumes, the ultimate in plumage displays are performed by the Common Peacock, Bird of Paradise, Lyrebird, and the Great Argus Pheasant. The displays of these species transform a bird's body into something resembling a fantastic, Martian flower or pulsating, nightmare sea anenome.

Sharp-Tailed Grouse (Tympanuchus phasianellus) *males gather at communal display grounds, called leks, and compete for mates by calling, jumping, inflating brightly colored air sacs, and performing ritualized movements. Females arrive, mate, then leave to lay eggs and rear young alone.*

Nest Display   In some species, such as the Magnificent Frigatebird, the male constructs a rough nest and displays upon it, waiting for a female to approach him. The male frigatebird makes himself more noticeable by inflating his softball-sized scarlet gular pouch. He points his bill upward and waits. An interested female will offer additional sticks for the nest. He will add these to his nest and the pair will mate and subsequently raise young. After mating, the vivid gular pouch will fade to orange and both parents will remain to guard the eggs and chicks from predation by cannibalistic neighboring frigatebirds.

Courtship Flights   Birds of prey perform courtship rituals aloft. Pairs circle high above their territory and acrobatically cartwheel through the air. A male hummingbird displays his plumage to a perched female. He executes U-shaped turns before her, displaying gemlike patches of iridescent feathers. Crests, ruffs, ear fans, and epaulets will be fluffed out and tail streamers will flutter as the male hummer hovers and turns, showing the glorious structural pigments of his feathers to the best effect. Quetzals and Pennant-wing Nightjars also have aerial plume displays, but White-throated Swifts are the only birds known to actually mate while aloft. The pairs tumble and slip through the air—a truly amazing performance.

Leks   In polygamous species such as the Prairie Chicken and Sharp-tailed Grouse, males often establish communal booming grounds or leks upon which they display. Females are attracted to the loud calls of the assembled males and thread their way through the lek, eventually choosing one displaying male to mate with. The females then disperse to raise their young while the males remain on the lek, strutting and calling to other females.

Male Sage Grouse (Centrocercus urophasianus) strut, fan their tails, and inflate their bright orange throat sacs to attract females and compete with other males. The throat sac deflates with a loud popping sound.

The Importance of Territory   In territorial birds, those who are not able to establish and hold a territory are unable to attract a mate and thus will not have the opportunity to breed. Ornithologists surmise that the females' evaluation of prospective mates is partially based upon the richness of their territory. Males will sing to identify territory, and border clashes between neighbors are frequent. A territorial male will physically drive out any competitor of the same species. At a campsite one spring day, I saw a male Northern Cardinal attacking his reflection in the rearview mirror of a pickup truck. He obviously thought that a rival had entered his territory. After watching his agitated attacks for more than an hour, someone in our camp had the good sense to cover the mirror with a towel. The cardinal lost all interest in the mirror and pickup truck once his illusory competitor had disappeared.

CHAPTER 3

Birdwatching Equipment

*T*he gear that a birder needs is relatively simple. Binoculars, field guide, and proper outdoor clothing are the basic items and many birders carry no more than these. Other birders load their packs and pockets with accessory equipment. What you take along will, in large part, depend upon the nature of your birdwatching excursion and your interests, but at the very least, you will need a good pair of binoculars.

Binoculars are the basic tool of the birdwatcher and the most essential piece of equipment. Binoculars not only bring distant objects into closer view, but they also enlarge them. Through binoculars you can see the eyelashes of a sleeping owl; binoculars resolve the small, black, white, and orange blob in the tree canopy into a Blackburnian Warbler; they reveal the identity of that large, red-tailed bird circling high overhead. Many of the best birders are tribal peoples from all over the world who are so keen-sighted that they don't need binoculars; however, most of us less-gifted birders feel blind and deprived when we try to see birds with the naked eye.

The spyglass that Long John Silver used to count cannons of the merchant ships he preyed upon is the great-grandfather of modern binoculars. If we were to draw the family tree of these aids to long-range observation, we would begin with Galileo's telescope (a collapsible monocular, focused by adjusting the distance between a pair of internal lenses), progress to opera and field glasses (pairs of low-power telescopes strapped side by side), and end with the prism binoculars readily available today. As well as ocular (near the eye) and objective (near the object) magnifying lenses, binoculars typically have pairs of internal prisms that permit the user to see a bigger, brighter image in a compact design. Porro prism binoculars have wide-set barrels and a stubby look, while the roof prism arrangement makes a slimmer, more elegant, more expensive binocular. Porro prisms usually have an external focusing mechanism while roof prisms have an internal focusing mechanism that allows the binoculars to be more waterproof. Whatever the style, binoculars allow you to better see at a distance because they both magnify objects and improve upon your natural binocular (two-eyed) vision.

Your binoculars will be your constant companion in the field. A fine pair will last your lifetime, while an inexpensive pair will be bumped out of alignment in a few months. An excellent pair will help you become a better birder and will be a treasured possession; a poor pair will test your patience and make you want to smash them on a rock. As a novice, you can do yourself a favor by learning the basics about binocs so that you can choose your own pair intelligently.

Binoculars: A Primer   This section will be more helpful if you have a pair of binocs in hand to examine, so, rummage around and find a pair (or look at the photo at left).

These Porro-prism 7 × 35 wide-angled glasses are affordable and would be useful for a beginning birder.

Magnifying Power

Examine the binoculars and find a pair of numbers separated by an ×, for example, 7×35, 7×50, 8×40, 10×50. The first number tells power of magnification; the second tells the diameter (in millimeters) of the objective lens. Thus, 8×42 binoculars have a magnifying power of 8 diameters and a clear objective lens aperture of 42 millimeters.

While 7×35 binoculars are the standard for birdwatching, they are not particularly high-powered glasses, but rather a compromise between efficiency of optics, practicality in the field, and cost. Although many seasoned birders prefer 10×50 binoculars, they are seldom the best choice for a beginner. They maximize hand shake, making some birders feel giddy and nauseous, and unless your neck, shoulder, and arm muscles are very strong, affordable 10×50s will feel like lead weights.

Field of View: Wide or Narrow?

Binoculars that are adequate for birding have a fairly wide field of view, that is, the amount of area you can see when the glasses are stationary. A wide field of view lets you both scan the horizon and follow moving birds with ease. Field of view depends upon the internal design of the binoculars, and although you won't find any number stamped on them to tell you how wide their field of view is, you can make a rough estimate based on their magnification. For instance, 7× glasses tend to have wider fields of view than 10× glasses. Test this feature to find a pair of glasses that suits you.

Mini roof-prisms are the lightest binoculars, but the narrow field of vision and low magnification often detract from their overall usefulness.

BIRD EQUIPMENT

Great Egrets (Casmerodius albus) *often feed by walking slowly through shallow water, searching for frogs, fish, and insects. They breed in marshes, but may often be spotted hunting in irrigation or drainage ditches.*

Depth of Field

Depth of field tells how thick (or deep) the plane of focus is. The degree of three-dimensionality of the binocular image is influenced by the distance between the objective lenses. The wider these lenses are set apart, the thicker the depth of field. The crooked design of porro prism binoculars allows their objective lenses to be set further apart than those of roof prism binoculars. Theoretically, porro prism binoculars should provide a deeper three-dimensional view.

Exit Pupil and Relative Brightness

Relative brightness measures the light-gathering ability of binoculars. Because their prisms and lenses gobble up light, the strength of a beam of light diminishes from 4 to 8 percent as it passes through a pair of binoculars. To compensate for this loss, the ideal pair of binoculars has an objective lens wide enough to admit a beam of light that will measure 5 mm in diameter as it leaves the ocular lens and enters the birder's eye. This measurement is called the exit pupil.

It is easy to determine the diameter of the exit pupil of a pair of binoculars. Divide the width of the objective lens by the magnification, or the second number by the first. Thus for 7×35 binoculars, 35 is divided by 7 to get an exit pupil diameter of 5 mm. Lens makers square this number to get the relative brightness of a pair of binoculars. Exit pupil size will become important when you're birding in poor light conditions. If you plan to bird at night, you will need 7×50s, which give a maximum exit pupil of 7.1 mm.

If you're wondering how the ideal exit pupil width of 5 mm is derived, consider that in total darkness the iris of the human eye can dilate to a maximum diameter of 7 mm; in intense, bright light it can constrict to a minimum diameter of 2 mm. Birding often takes place at dawn or at dusk, when your pupil typically enlarges to 5 mm in diameter. Binoculars with exit pupils less than 5 mm or relative brightness less than 25 are not effective in these low light conditions.

Eye Relief

Eye relief does not involve applying soothing cucumber compresses to strained eyes, but rather refers to the distance from the ocular lens to the exit pupil, where the image is refocused for view. Binoculars typically have an eye relief of 9–10 mm, meaning that the image exiting the binoculars reaches the birder's eye and is in perfect focus 9–10 mm beyond the ocular lens.

Bohemian Waxwings (Bombycila garrulus) *form nomadic flocks in winter, often together with Cedar Waxwings* (Bombycilla cedrorum) *and American Robins* (Turdus migratorius). *They are found in coniferous and mixed woodlands.*

Eye relief becomes a problem only if you wear eyeglasses, because these keep your eyes from getting as close as 9–10 mm from the ocular lens. The eyeglass barrier prevents you from seeing the entire field of view. To solve this problem, binocular manufacturers sell extended eye-relief binoculars (sometimes called "B" models) that have an eye relief of 15 mm and rubber sleeves around the ocular lenses. The rubber sleeves are extended when eyeglasses are not worn and are rolled down when they are. There are two common misconceptions about these sleeves. Some think that they are intended to protect eyeglasses from being scratched by binoculars; others think that any binocs with rubber sleeves are specially designed for eyeglass wearers.

Extended Eye Relief

If you wear eyeglasses, request Model B, or extended eye relief, binoculars. Do not trust the presence of rubber eye sleeves to indicate this feature. To ensure that you are seeing the entire field of view instead of just part of it, try this test. With your glasses on, roll down the sleeves and examine a scene. Do you see a complete circle surrounded by a black rim? If the glasses are correct for your interpupillary distance and you see a pair of circles or somewhat overlapping circles, your eye is too far away from the exit pupil to see the entire field of view. Reject any binoculars that give this effect even when they are correctly adjusted for your interpupillary distance.

Evaluating Binoculars: Caveat Emptor

My best advice to a beginner is to borrow or rent and use binoculars before you buy them. A season, or even a few days, in the field with that pair gathering dust in Aunt Maude's closet will give you time to learn more about binoculars in general, and what you want in a pair. You will develop an instinct for the proper weight and width of field of view. Ask other birders for their recommendations and, better yet, test their binoculars in the field. Look for binoculars in pawn shops and secondhand stores. And when you do decide to buy your own binoculars, get the highest-quality equipment you can afford.

What Brand?

Avoid "bargains" and "specials" when buying binoculars, because with optical equipment, you tend to get what you pay for. Reliable name brands tend to be higher quality, but as a beginner, you will not be familiar with all brands of binoculars and will be bewildered by

Bird nests screened by foliage in summer are often easy to spot in winter. Binoculars can provide a close-up view.

the array of unfamiliar names. Help is available. The staff of the Laboratory of Ornithology at Cornell University in Ithaca, New York, evaluates models of binoculars for their "birdability." They include affordable binoculars, as well as models in higher price ranges. *The Living Bird Quarterly* will mail you a reprint of the latest evaluation if you send a self-addressed, stamped envelope (see page 126).

Be sure to examine a number of different makes and models of binoculars to determine your preferences. Busy stores are probably the worst places to conduct a thoughtful evaluation of optical equipment, but they may be your only choice. Give yourself plenty of time and go in the daytime so that you can step outside and compare the glasses in natural light. Ask to see a range of prices, manufacturers, and powers. Include top-of-the-line models by Nikon, Zeiss, Swift, Bausch & Lomb, and Leitz, and use the Binocular Evaluation Checklist on page 124 to help you find the best pair for you.

Interpupillary Distance

Adjust the binoculars to the width of your eyes by gently pressing the barrels inward or pulling them outward. The barrels will be in proper alignment for your eyes when the image resolves into a single, round field surrounded by a rim of black. Reject any binocs in which your view is a pair of portholes swimming in blackness or a pair of partially joined circles.

Aquatic habitats abound with birds. Birding from a canoe is a quiet way to approach and watch many species. Make sure equipment is kept in a waterproof case when not in use.

Focusing

Binoculars that are suitable for birding have a center focusing mechanism. Do not buy binoculars with individually focused barrels, because focusing one eye and then the other is too time-consuming, especially when a prime specimen has just taken flight.

To set the binoculars for your eyes, cover the right objective lens with a lens cap or close your right eye. Now, find a distant object and focus the left lens using the central focusing knob or bar. Then, open your right eye and focus using the right ocular adjustment. Once this is done, any subsequent focusing will be made using only the central focus. While you are focusing, check the ease with which the focusing knob moves. Does it grind or does it move smoothly? Reject any binocs that slide out of focus by themselves.

Lens Quality

Lens quality is very important and takes concentration to determine. Use the binoculars to examine something that has lots of vertical and horizontal lines; a piece of newspaper tacked to the wall is perfect. Is the center of the field focused or blurry? Is there blurring at the edges? Take time to examine carefully. Poor lenses often have imperfections that distort the scene.

Now, imagine that there is a clock face superimposed on the scene and carefully check all twelve hours of the clock for blurring, distortion, and curving of horizontal and vertical lines. Reject any binoculars that show lens imperfections.

Brightness of Image

Hold the binoculars by their objective lenses and tilt them back and forth until you catch a

The beard of a male Wild Turkey (Meleagris gallopavo) *helps him to orient himself over the female, aligning his cloaca with hers.*

reflection from the lenses and prisms within. Because glass absorbs light, the binocular image tends to be darker than the real thing. To counter this problem, interior optics are coated to minimize light loss and reduce glare. If your binocs have coated optics, you will see a rich blue, purple, or amber reflection as you tilt them. Manufacturers sometimes skimp and coat only the exterior lenses. Uncoated interior lenses will show a bright, harsh reflection or white spots will appear within the colored reflections. When you've examined the objective lenses, turn the glasses around and inspect the ocular lenses in the same manner.

Other Considerations

Compare Porro prism and roof prism designs to determine your preference. Hang the binoculars around your neck and see how heavy they feel. Hold them up to your eyes and, without moving, stare at the scene for two minutes. Are your arms aching? Are your wrists trembling?

The Dicksissel (Spiza americana) is a species of fields, meadows, and grasslands. Males have a black bib and prefer to sing from a conspicuous perch. Females are more secretive and less colorful, and therefore harder to spot.

Minibinoculars may be the perfect compromise for you. Choose the most powerful, most lightweight glasses you can afford. Try them outside and observe the width of the field of view as well as the brightness of image. Finally, look for these added features:

- rubbery-plastic armor coating to help minimize damage in the field—sooner or later you will drop your binocs

- a case hard enough to protect your binoculars when someone accidentally sits on them

- a rain guard for the ocular lenses

- removable caps for all four lenses

- waterproofing or water resistance

After a few weeks of use, you may want to replace the manufacturer's narrow neck strap with something wider and more comfortable. Many birders prefer the soft, foam-cushioned straps sold in camera stores. While you are there, buy lens paper to clean your binoculars.

USING BINOCULARS

"Where? Where? I can't find it."

Finding a bird with binoculars is a major obstacle for most novice birders. A typical scenario goes something like this:

> At the edge of a woodlot a small bird is singing in the crown of a leafless tree. To the naked eye the bird is a mobile, dark blob about "two o'clock." An eager, first-time birder spots the blob, recognizes it as a possible bird, and then looks down as he lifts his binocs to his eyes. After fumbling a minute to focus, he finds himself searching a maze of twigs and branches where he thought the bird was perched. Try as he might, he cannot locate it. He scans up and down, left and right, but cannot see what the others in his party are exclaiming about. The motion of his binoculars makes him feel faintly nauseous, but our beginner keeps silent, not wanting to seem stupid. Soon his arms and neck are aching and, enthusiasm dampened, he lowers his binocs in time to see the mystery bird fly off.

It takes practice to gain skill in focusing binoculars and in locating objects with them. Birds are particularly frustrating because they tend to fly away just as you get them in focus. The following pair of pointers will help solve the beginner's initial problems (but keep in mind that there is no substitute for practice in the field).

Large, relatively sedentary birds like these basking Anhingas (Anhinga anhinga) *are easy for beginning birders to find and get into focus.*

RULE 1: Use Both Hands

Good birders always carry their binoculars in both hands in the field, especially when a lot is happening. So, until you have mastered the use of your binocs and can afford to be more relaxed, follow the experts' example. Hang your binocs around your neck and carry them slightly raised or "at the ready." You will be surprised at how much this habit will improve your skill in birding. While others are fumbling to grab their glasses, you will be focusing.

RULE 2: Don't Look Away

Once you spot a bird, keep your eyes on it. If it flies to another nearby perch, follow it with your eyes and to a better vantage point. Then, without transferring your gaze from the bird, lift your binocs to your eyes. When you focus your glasses, the bird should be in the center of your field of view. It is imperative that you do not shift your gaze to the binoculars as you bring them up. You may have only a few seconds to see a bird; if you look away, you will have to relocate it.

At this point you are ready to begin to learn to use binoculars. The following exercise is intended to give beginners a taste of birdwatching, but it is sufficiently complex that even intermediate birders will enjoy it.

PIGEON BEHAVIOR

Objectives Originally from Europe, domestic pigeons (also called Rock Doves and Rock Pigeons) now have a nearly worldwide distribution. Even though millions of people see pigeons everyday, only specialists understand the set of postures and sounds that these ground-dwelling birds use to communicate with each other. This first field trip exercise involves seeking out flocks of pigeons and observing them, with and without binoculars.

The ubiquitous pigeon, or Rock Dove (Columba livia), *makes a good subject for beginning birdwatchers.*

Your aim will be to practice using binoculars, to sharpen your powers of observation, and to begin to learn to record what you see. This exercise is not birding, per se, but over the years I have found that it gets the beginner immediately involved and over those first awkward days in the field in a painless, sometimes hilarious way. You will be amazed and amused at the bird behaviors that have escaped your notice all these years.

Equipment

Binoculars, field notebook and pencil, bird field guide (see page 75), warm clothes if necessary. Any pocket-sized notebook will do as a field notebook for this exercise, but if you prefer, see page 77–81 for a discussion of notes and note-taking.

Procedure

Locate a flock of pigeons. Look on ledges for flocks that are basking in a warm, sheltered spot or in nearby parks for flocks that are feeding. Look for roosts beneath overpasses and flocks that congregate on the ridges of barns. Watch the effect of your presence on the flock and stay far enough away so that you don't disturb the birds' natural actions. Like most other birds, pigeons have two activity periods, sunrise until about 11:00 a.m. and 4:00 p.m. until sunset. Pigeons tend to rest at midday.

Sighting

With the sun at your back, practice spotting a single bird and then sighting it in your binocs. Choose different pigeons at different distances and repeat the following sequence of action—spot, sight, focus, observe—until they blend into a single, fluid reaction. This will take some practice.

Pigeon Appearance

Locate a resting pigeon and, using binocs, make detailed observations of its color. Note colors of plumage on head, neck, breast, back, belly, wings, and tail as well as the colors of

Rock Doves (Columba livia) *are sexually active for nine months of the year.*

eyes, legs, and feet. Does it have eyelashes? Jot your observations down in your field notebook and then check your bird guide to make sure you have seen all the field marks (distinctive body shape, size, color) that distinguish the Rock Dove, as ornithologists name *Columba livia*. Note this sequence: Jot down observations first and then consult your field guide. Try to see as much as possible. Make rough sketches that show color and pattern. Don't worry about being a lousy artist. No one but you will ever see these field notes, you can draw your pigeon as a ball with feet and wings. The important thing is to draw it and label your drawing. We will discuss more formal field notes later. For now, observe and record and try to do the best job you can. Remember that most of us have been trained to ignore most of what goes on around us. As a birder, you have to learn to see, and this takes much practice.

Size

Scan the pigeon again to firmly fix in your mind the concept of "pigeon-sized." You will need this idea later.

Sex

Male and female pigeons look very similar, and only pigeon fanciers and real experts can tell the sexes apart solely by external appearance. But male pigeons will advertise their presence using characteristic displays to attract potential mates.

Your next objective is to observe a courting male pigeon; because pigeons are sexually active almost year-round, this should not be difficult. Look for a bird that is ruffling its neck feathers, lowering its head, and turning around in full or half circles. Although females also do this bowing display, it is primarily done by males. To make sure that your pigeon is a male, watch for a tail-dragging display in which the male completes the bowing display and then fans his tail and drags it along the ground. The male will give a characteristic soft cooing call as he drags his tail. Bowing is often followed by tail dragging, and if your bird does both displays, you are undoubtedly watching a sexually interested male Rock Dove. Males usually bow and tail-drag repeatedly, so you will have plenty of time to watch and then sketch the displays so that you don't forget them.

Couples

As you watch your flock of pigeons with unaided eyes, look for pairs of birds that seem to be running among the flock or away from it. It will look as though the second bird is chasing the first. This is the driving display, and in it the female will be followed by the male.

Female Reaction

Study the actions of a female pigeon being courted by a bowing, tail-dragging male. It may seem as though she is ignoring him and continuing to feed, but watch carefully to see if she is actually picking anything from the ground as she pecks. Often she is only mechanically pecking. The driving display often follows the female's pecking without eating.

Copulation

Pigeons are not reticent birds, and even on busy streets copulations are frequent. Watch the female of a courting pair as she allows the male to briefly stand on her back and bring his downward-pumping tail towards hers. This is often accompanied by vigorous wing flapping as the male struggles to simultaneously maintain his balance and bring his cloaca into contact with the female's for introduction of sperm. Do the birds coo during copulation? Do they shut their eyes? What behaviors precede and follow it? Watch several copulating pairs and record your observations.

Wing-Clapping Flight

Listen for the clapping sound made by pigeon wings as they hit together on the upstroke. Everyone has heard this flat clapping sound, but few know that bird behaviorists believe that to pigeons it advertises the presence of a sexually active male or female. It is given as a bird enters or exits a flock.

TELESCOPES AND TRIPODS

While binoculars are the birdwatcher's essential optical equipment, even with binocs many waterfowl and shorebirds are too far away to be more than mere specks in the distance. A spotting 'scope brings them close enough to enjoy. As with binoculars, investigate the market carefully before buying. Birders love to brag about their 'scopes and tripods and you'll get lots of free advice and recommendations. The best 'scopes are waterproof, have zoom lenses, and large objective lenses (at least 60 mm), and magnify between 15× and 45×. They also cost as much as two or three mortgage payments. Serviceable, less expensive models are available. Before you buy, check the difference between offset and straight eyepieces to determine your preference. If you plan to try photography, you will want a camera attachment. If price is no object, you will want to purchase a higher-power ocular lens. *The Living Bird Quarterly* will mail you its evaluation of 'scopes if you send a self-addressed, stamped envelope (see page 126).

Winter birding in the North can be very exciting. Leafless trees make birds easier to spot and many species form feeding flocks after the breeding season. Just make sure to bundle up, layering clothing for extra warmth.

A good tripod is lightweight yet sturdy. It has spiked legs that extend and lock at the flick of a lever without manual tugging and twisting. Other standard features are a crank-turned central rod with gears to elevate the head of the tripod and a gearshiftlike rod that is swiveled to point and turn to lock.

FIELD GUIDES

Buying Your First Guide   Prior to the 1933 publication of Roger Tory Peterson's classic *A Field Guide to the Birds*, birdwatchers had few visual aids to help them sort out the birds they saw. Adapted from techniques used to identify warplanes at a distance, the Peterson method simplifies bird identification by boiling down the mass of details of bird appearance into characteristics that can be spotted at a distance. These "field marks" include overall body size, size and shape of the wings, tail, bill, legs, and feet, and color and pattern. Behavioral clues and song are also important. While the Peterson *Guide* now has many competitors, it is the standard by which all others are judged.

A large bookstore will have several bird field guides from which to choose. All have color pictures, pointers for identification, range maps, and indexes. Size is important. Make sure that the guide you purchase is small enough to fit into your jacket pocket (approximately 4 by 7 inches or 10 by 17.5 cm) and that it has a sewn (not glued) binding so that it doesn't quickly deteriorate under hard use in the field. Sooner or later you and your field guide will get soaking wet—your canoe will tip, you will fall into a stream, you will get caught in a downpour. As you are drying out, remember to dry your field guide—if possible, put absorbent paper (toilet tissue works well) between the pages while they are still damp. Otherwise, the pages will stick together and your book will be spoiled.

Because bird taxonomy and nomenclature are constantly being revised, it is best to purchase the latest edition available. Be sure to choose one that is specific for your region. Comprehensive field guides that show all of the birds in the country or on the continent tend to be more confusing to beginners than more restricted regional guides. While birds do occasionally stray out of their normal geographic ranges—for example, a Green-tailed Towhee native to chaparral of the southwest appearing at a bird feeder in Ohio, or a Lesser Spotted Woodpecker visiting northern England—this is uncommon and a regional guide will be all that a beginner initially needs. Most birders have a library of guides and carry a personal favorite into the field. (For a partial listing of available field guides, see page 125.)

Homework   Buying your bird guide is only a first step. At home you will want to read the introductory chapters and browse through the book, familiarizing yourself with its organization and studying pictures of birds you are likely to encounter. Most guides are arranged in phylogenetic order, starting with the most primitive birds and ending with the most advanced, crows, jays, and their relatives. Peterson's guides, however, follow their own organizational scheme. Page through the species accounts and read those of birds you know. Study the introductory sections about field marks, and don't be daunted by the number of birds you've never seen. Imagine seeing a Saw Whet Owl or Blackburnian Warbler for the first time!

Good birders become good birders by studying their field guides. Preparation at home is one of the things that will transform a raw beginner into a better birder. Pretend that your field guide is a novel and read it from cover to cover. Study the illustrations. Put a copy in the bathroom or on your bedside table. To a great extent, your success as a birder will depend upon what you expect to see. Your expectations will largely be based upon your knowledge of what is possible.

FIELD NOTES

Experienced birders fall into two categories: those who keep records and those who don't. Record keepers tend to be either listers or note-takers. I encourage you to take notes.

Taking notes gives you a framework for future observations and organizes your thinking. Writing a summary of your day's observations allows you to reflect upon what you've seen; you develop sharper perceptions and begin to think about birds and their habits instead of merely chasing them in the field, looking for novelty. You begin to see patterns in nature and ask questions about them. End-of-season analysis of your notes puts things into perspective for future birding trips and future seasons. Finally, it's satisfying to look back on a year's worth of notes and remember details of days in the field that would otherwise disappear in the rush of more immediate events.

Northern Orioles (Icterus galbula) *weave a hanging basket nest attached to a slender tree branch.*

A note-taker in action. Birdwatching can be recreation, relaxation, education, competition, and science—you don't need an excuse to enjoy it.

Write and Remember If you're like me, you tend to forget things. While others I know can remember the minutest details of events that occurred years ago, much of what happened a few days ago—even yesterday—is a vague blur to me. In a month, I will have forgotten almost everything that has recently happened. But if I've written it down, it is mine forever. This simple fact is the basis of my cardinal rule with field notes: Write and remember; memory forgets. Or, to put it another way: Write it down when you see it. Your memory is worse than you think it is.

In the pigeon-watching exercise, I suggested that you use a small, pocket-sized notebook to record your observations. This field notebook is essential, and you will have to test several designs before finding one that suits you. I have tried small notebooks of every description and have learned that hard covers are a great help when you're writing or sketching in the field. For me, the perfect notebook is about the size of a field guide. This has the disadvantage of being too large for a breast pocket but the advantage of larger pages. You must also decide whether you prefer a horizontally opening book or one that opens vertically.

Basic Notes   The following information will be included in each field notebook entry:

- date, time, and weather conditions
- locality
- objective
- travel directions
- field companions

What you jot down after this is up to you. I usually keep a running list of birds sighted (with names underlined with a wavy line) to make it easy to see them later. I also add behavioral observations and details that interest me. I try to write neatly, but sloppy notes are better than none and mine are usually cryptic—unreadable to anyone else. Because my field notebook is often in my jacket pocket, it tends to get filled with grocery lists, phone numbers, and other odd bits of information. I glue a small manilla envelope to the inside back cover for business cards, receipts, and maps. A large rubber band around the front cover holds the book open to the page I'm using and also provides a secure place for a pen or pencil.

Field notes are not meant to be finished works, but rather the raw material for your field journal, which you can write up at your leisure. While field notes are rough-and-ready, field journal accounts are more polished. Old

A page from my field journal for 1990.

field notebooks are filed in case you might need them in the future; it is your field journal that you will read ten years from now. The ideal birdwatching journal account will instantly recapture a day in the field.

I prefer to make my own field journal instead of using a purchased bound, blank book. Because I want my record to last, I buy large sheets of 100 percent rag, acid-free, hot-pressed, smooth-sur-faced paper from an art supply store and cut them into pieces that are 9 by 6 inches (22.5 by 15 cm). These small sheets are punched to fit a 3-ring loose-leaf binder and ruled to provide a one-inch (2.5-cm) left margin and a half-inch (1.2-cm) top margin. I usually prepare 100 sheets at a time and my current yearly field journals have about 300 pages. At the end of the year, I reread my journal, make an alphabetical index, and bind all of the pages into a book. Although I began watching birds over thirty years ago, keeping organized field notes and a field journal is a relatively new pursuit and I have only bound field journals for the last four years. I enjoy rereading them and remembering other seasons, and within limits, try to make my journal accounts as complete as possible. I wish I had learned how to keep field notes and a field journal when I first started birding thirty years ago.

The method that I follow is not original but it is based on the system of journal keeping devised by Joseph Grinnell of the Museum of Vertebrate Zoology at the University of California, Berkeley, and described by S.G. Herman (see page 125). Dr. Herman's Naturalist's Field Journal is an instructive, easy-to-read treatise on how to keep field records. It amplifies the brief ideas given here and presents alternatives.

Life Lists   The most familiar method of keeping track of the birds seen, and the starting place for most birders, is the life list. In its simplest form, this is just a list, sometimes recorded in a bird guide, of the species a birder sees in a lifetime. Others make more elaborate lists that detail the cir-cumstances surrounding the sighting of "life" birds or "lifers" (species seen for the first time). But this is just the beginning of variations on the theme of listing. There are even computer programs that help generate impressive-looking yearly summaries. The life list has a tendency to sprout a variety of subordinate, imaginative lists: "vacation list," "backyard list," "feeder list," "all-of-the-birds-in-the-apple-tree list," "birds-seen-on-the-drive-to-work list." The passion for listing leads a few birders to make the life list their major interest in birding; studying the fascinating details of behavior as well as the beauty and comedy of birdlife can become subordinate to getting another species. While extreme listing can engender fierce competition and one-upmanship, in its benign form, listing is a minor madness that allows birders to monitor their performance in the field as well as keep track of changes in bird populations.

One variation of the life list that has become a popular fund-raising event with many bird clubs is the Birdathon. On a specified day, teams of birders take to the field to see and list as many birds as they can within a given time. The birders represent sponsors who have pledged a certain dollar amount for each species recorded. These friendly competitions not only raise funds for local bird clubs and for conservation, but they also generate data on species abundance, breeding, and distribution.

The Christmas Count is the grandmother of the Birdathon. It originated in 1900 when Frank M. Chapman, then chairman of the Department of Ornithology of the American Museum of Natural History and a founder of the Audubon Society, and twenty-six of his friends spent Christmas Day in the field, counting birds. The annual Christmas Count, which doesn't necessarily have to coincide with Christmas Day, has grown to a census of global proportions. Volunteers generate information about range expansions and contractions, fluctuations in population numbers, and wintering populations of birds.

Sketching   "I can't draw," most beginning birders insist. "Especially not something as complicated as a bird." Well, the good news is that you don't have to make perfect renderings of birds you see. Simple sketches will do. Although sketching is not always practical, birders should try to make some field sketches on each trip. The process of sketching is what is important—it transforms your powers of observation. People who draw tend to see more, see better, and remember more of what they see than those who do not draw.

Hummingbirds build nests of plant fibers, which they bind with spider silk. The Rufous Hummingbird (Selasphorus rufus) *breeds farther north than any other hummer, reaching Southern Alaska.*

While American birders tend to feel naked without a field guide to confirm their identifications, most European and British birders will go into the field with only binoculars and sketch pad. The bird book is left in the car or at home. Try this system and see how it works for you. I've found that it's remarkably freeing.

THE WELL-DRESSED BIRDER

Binoculars, field guide, field notebook, and pen or pencil are the basic equipment for birding, but because you will be outdoors for hours at a time, it is also necessary to have suitable, comfortable clothing. The weather and the season will dictate what you wear. A few suggestions follow.

Cold Weather   Foil the cold with many layers. Long underwear that wicks moisture away from your skin (not cotton; it absorbs moisture) and thus keeps your skin dry and warm is a worthwhile investment. I've tried silk, cotton/wool, and polypropylene of various sorts and recommend Patagonia's Expedition Underwear long underwear. It's expensive, but nearly indestructible and wonderfully snug. It may be too warm and thick for some birders. Your field jacket deserves careful thought. For really cold weather, it should be large enough to allow you to wear several thin, woolen sweaters, a down vest, a turtleneck, and long underwear without feeling constricted and exhausted before you leave the house. There should be plenty of room for your arms to move. Your jacket should have lots of pockets; at least two should be large enough to hold both field guide and field notebook without straining seams. Birds see colors and their vision is far superior to ours; avoid bright colors—think dead leaf. Have a limited budget? Investigate jackets at Army surplus stores. Have lots of cash? Buy a Gore-Tex™ jacket.

You will need sturdy, waterproof boots that allow you to safely clamber over boulders and down slippery slopes. In winter, boots

When spring comes, dedicated birders find themselves irresistibly drawn to the margins of marshes—finally the migration is on!

should be insulated. Wear two pairs of socks (thin and thick to avoid blisters), and put an extra pair in your pack just in case your feet get wet.

Even if you hate hats, tuck a cap or skier's earband into your pocket. It may save your ears from frostbite.

Gloves or mittens become critical in winter birding. I wear a pair of thin, cotton gloves (scrounged at flea markets) in the fall and a pair of thin, woolen mittens inside thicker ones when it's really cold. Try hunter's mittens that have one split palm to allow your fingers out to focus binocs or 'scope.

Warm Weather   A lightweight, long-sleeved field jacket or a lightweight long-sleeved shirt will protect you from insects and sun. Sturdy walking shoes are a good alternative to field boots in warm weather. A broad-brimmed or billed cap will keep the sun out of your eyes. In areas where you may encounter ticks or chiggers, wear light-colored or khaki pants. As you dress for the field, tuck the cuffs of your trousers inside your socks; tuck your shirt inside your trousers. Any ticks will be forced to climb up your pant legs where their dark color will be conspicuous and they can be quickly removed and dispatched.

Vade mecum
In all seasons, a backpack or fanny pack with the following equipment makes birding trips more comfortable.

- lunch, canteen or thermos, salt and pepper

- health and hygiene aids: tissues, antihistamine, insect repellent, sunscreen or tanning lotion, lip balm, a few Band-Aids™, Ace™ tensor bandage, aspirin, breath mints, small mirror, safety pins

- essential field equipment: hand lens, thermometer, knife, compass, snakebite kit, plastic bags

- nonessential but occasionally indispensable: mini-flashlight, roll of waxed twine, tape measure, whistle

- extra pen and pencil

- essential if rain is likely: an ankle-length poncho or other compact rain gear

SEEING BIRDS

Seeing birds is largely a matter of being observant and quiet. The second quality is easier to achieve. Birds have much better eyes than humans and usually see us before we see them. Birds tend to be fearless and trusting, however, and if we don't frighten them with quick, big gestures and boisterous behavior, they will often allow us to get quite close. One habit to break is lifting your binocs to your eyes with a large, abrupt movement. Hold them up and ready; lift them smoothly.

Watch how experienced birders act in the field. They usually speak quietly, if at all, and never point to a bird. Because many birds will flush if you point at them, birders have developed the nearly universal system of mentally superimposing a clock face upon a tree or shrub to help locate a bird that someone else wants to see. Although birds don't always perch at the clock hours, it is easier to find a Rose-breasted Grosbeak at "nine o'clock" than to follow the mental gymnastics of "find the fork of the tree and go up until the branch of the other tree crosses it, just about where that dead limb is, then go over about a foot, and..." By this time, the bird is gone.

While novice birders tend to chatter, experienced birders are close-mouthed. They walk quietly and stop often to listen. Size of group also affects noise level, and you can hear many big groups of birders long before you see them. People go on bird walks for many reasons; some even go to see birds. Large groups often have a convivial outing, but, unless the leader is a expert at crowd control, individuals tend to see less. To my way of thinking, three or four people is the ideal size for a birding party.

Keeping quiet in the field allows a birder to hear bird songs, notes, and calls. Most birders who recognize bird songs will commonly hear many more birds than actually see and recognition and identification of a song by a competent observer counts as much as having seen the bird. Indeed, some birds, like the Red-eyed Vireo (often called "The Preacher" in the

Birds have to eat even in bitter weather, so it's never too cold for birding.

southern United States because of its continuous, repetitive song) are shy and seldom seen, but are regularly heard.

Although I try to be a good observer, I know that I often see only a small fraction of what goes on in the field. To see and hear new things and to see and hear more is a constant challenge. My field classes have taught me the importance of preparation prior to fieldwork; to a great extent, people see and hear what they know about.

Seeing More Birds   Studying your field guide is only one way to help yourself see more birds. Here are other things to try:

• If you really can't tell a Bluebird from a Blue Jay, buy a bird book meant for children and immerse yourself in easy identifications. Try a bird coloring book (no one has to know for whom you are buying those colored pencils) or a small Golden or Audubon *First Guides*. You will be surprised at how quickly and painlessly this method of learning works.

You don't need to go far to find birds to watch. A nearby park will provide plenty of opportunities.

• Let the birds come to you. Find a good place, bring a stool, and sit for a few hours.

• Think food. Birds are attracted to blossoming trees and pollinating insects in spring, fruits in summer and fall.

• If the birds are shy, hide. Lean against a tree so your silhouette is not so plainly visible, or seek cover.

• If a bird stops singing, stand still and try to answer its call.

- Choose a mentor. An experienced birder may find your enthusiasm refreshing and respond with birding techniques and favorite, secret locations. This contact could be the start of a treasured friendship.

- Go birding with more experienced birders.

- When a bird is singing, try to find it. Then scan for nearby, silent individuals.

- Don't dismiss all members of a flock as the same species. Examine all individuals. You often turn up odd warblers or sparrows this way.

- Learn to recognize bird sounds. Buy recordings (cassette tapes and CDs are finally available) of bird songs and calls and listen to them over and over. You will soon begin to recognize the common birds.

- Watch for movement.

- Scan with your binoculars as well as with unaided eyes.

- Vary your observation times. In fair or warm weather, small land birds are most active at early morning and at dusk; they are active all day when it is cold and wet. Water birds tend to rest at high tide and feed at low tide.

- Try owling.

- Join a bird club. Attend lectures and field trips to areas you might not visit on your own.

- Take a bird course at your local high school adult education program, college, Audubon Society, zoo, natural history museum, or Y.

- Bring your binoculars along on a trip to the zoo.

- Buy a second pair of binocs and keep them in your car.

- Take a birding vacation.

- Read.

The Birding Year   Although few birders are out in the cold, to my way of thinking, winter is the ideal time for beginners to start birding. Not only are there fewer baffling birds around, but the beginner can learn the winter residents before the migrants arrive. Once spring comes, the beginner will be able to disregard the now familiar calls of the residents and home in on calls and songs of novel migrants. And, of course few things are as beautiful as a quiet woods after a snow. January nights are for owling. By all means, go birding in winter. There is lots to see.

Cactus Wrens (Campylorynchus brunneicapillus) *weave nests in thorny shrubs and large cactus, sites which predators find hard to reach.*

Spring has the most birds and is at once the most confusing and the most exciting season. Warblers arrive in their typical waves, and on a good day, a blossoming tree will be full of small, active, brilliantly colored birds. Many of the males make themselves conspicuous by singing, usually high, insecty-sounding, or twittering songs. Warbler time is the busiest season of the birding year, with many birders going into the field every day, avidly trying to see new warblers. Warblers are addictive and challenging: this is the season when birding can become an obsession. Spring is also the time for residents to establish territories; males (and females in some species) sing to attract mates. Pairing, courtship, and nesting can be observed.

After the rush and bustle of spring, summer is much quieter and birds are harder to find. Song is usually restricted to early morning or dusk. Parent birds build nests, incubate, and rear their young; some have two broods in years when food is abundant. Summer is a good time to study bird tapes, learn the habits of nesting birds, and watch as fledglings take their first wobbly flights. Immature plumages

In summer, the Gray-Cheeked Thrush (Catharus mimus) breeds in Northern Canada. In autumn the birds migrate through the central and eastern United States to wintering grounds as far south as Peru.

are a challenge. If you travel in summer, birding trips can be a welcome diversion on a vacation, adding exotic species to the lists you keep.

In the autumn, a protracted reverse migration begins in July with tiny warblers and extends until December with the last waterfowl. Bird numbers are swollen from the addition of young, but males of many species have molted their bright mating plumage and appear as drab as females. Birds are abundant in autumn, but often birding is quieter; fewer species sing on their southward migration. Autumn is the time to go hawkwatching.

CHAPTER 4

Finding Birds

*B*irds are everywhere you look—gathering at the feeder in the backyard, soaring above the highway, pecking in the park, swooping down on the beach—so why should you need information on where to look for birds? The answer lies in the fact that birds are adapted to specific habitats, from mountain streams to sage brush flats to sandy seashores to rain forest canopies. Thus, if you wish to see certain types of birds that do not live in your neighborhood, you must know where those particular birds are likely to be found. Your field guide will outline the known habitats of each bird listed, and is an excellent place to start.

HABITAT WATCHING

As you become a more experienced birder, the stereotypical behavior of each bird species will become increasingly apparent. Because of their highly specific food requirements, members of some different species tend to be found in the same places. For example, Rufoussided Towhees and Brown Thrashers typically forage in the leaf litter alongside White-throated Sparrows; Northern and Louisiana Waterthrushes are always seen along creeks, streams, and at lake side. At first you may be overwhelmed by the volume of bird species to learn; later patterns will begin to emerge. Eventually, you will know where to find most of the common bird species in your area.

Where to Look For Birds   Birds may be everywhere, but each species exhibits a specific need for a particular habitat. For many species, habitat requirements are somewhat flexible, and the birds can adapt to a variety of conditions. For many others, the required habitat is a very specific (and often shrinking) niche in the ecosystem.

The adaptable American Robin, for instance, is equally at home under the eaves of a house, in the bushes in the backyard, at the edge of the field, in a patch of woods near a stream, in the park, in the garden, or in the suburbs. The Kirtland's Warbler, on the other hand, will breed only in a northern stand of jack pines, five to twenty-two years old; the site must have sandy soil, a stream wandering through, and a few grassy clearings, ideally created by wildfires.

There are American Robins in abundance but perhaps only two hundred breeding pairs

Look for the Red-Breasted Nuthatch (Sitta canadensis) *in stands of coniferous trees throughout the United States and southern Canada. The species forages on tree trunks, often moving head down, looking for small insects under bark.*

of Kirtland's Warblers. Loss of habitat contributes significantly to the list of major threats to bird life on the planet.

Food is the single most important habitat requirement. The diet of some species is so specific that an otherwise suitable habitat will be abandoned if the required food is unavailable. Water, nesting sites and materials, adequate space for establishing territories, correct temperature, humidity, amount of light, precipitation—all of these and populations of predators and parasites help to define suitable habitat.

Many different species occupy the same habitat, but each occupies a different niche in the system. In a typically mixed woodland habitat, for instance, a myriad of avian species will be found sharing the same space. Each has a separate "job." Warblers search the canopy for insects, while towhees and robins find theirs in the fallen leaves. Wrens move through the vegetation and fallen branches on the forest floor, while nuthatches work up and down the tree trunks and branches.

The Little Green Heron (Butorides virescens) is one of the smallest herons. Look for it at the edge of ponds, streams, marshes—nearly any body of water—standing motionless, seeking small fish, then making a quick strike.

Birders use their knowledge of preferred habitats to seek out particular species and, very often, to help with identification. Some species are so specific in their habitat preferences that the fact of where the bird is seen can serve to differentiate it from similar species. The five species of empidonax flycatchers offer the best example of using habitat to identify similar species. All five of these birds are nearly impossible to separate by appearance alone, but their habitats are very different: You will find the Acadian Flycatcher in deciduous woods, particularly beech trees, and in wooded swamps; the Yellow-bellied Flycatcher in coniferous woods and bogs; the Least Flycatcher on farms, in orchards, and in open woods; the Willow Flycatcher in wet and dry thickets, brushy pastures, and willows; and the Alder Flycatcher in alder swamps and wet thickets near water.

Birding Hot Spots　　Places of suitable habitats where large concentrations of birds may be seen during migration and/or breeding season are called "hot spots" in birding circles. Hot spots are typically located along established migratory flyways, coastal waterways, swamps, wintering grounds, and so forth. Many such habitats are protected within parks and wildlife refuges.

A SAMPLING OF BIRDING HOT SPOTS

United States

Alaska attracts birds that are seen nowhere else in North America. Southeastern Alaska boasts the largest population of Bald Eagles. Glacier Bay is the meeting place of thousands of shorebirds, while the Chilkat Eagle Gathering attracts over 4,000 eagles to a 4-mile (6.4-km) stretch of the Chilkat River each year when the salmon run. The Kenai Peninsula in south-central Alaska hosts such intriguing species as Horned Puffins, Oyster-Catchers, Black-legged Kittiwakes, murrelets, and more. Uncountable numbers of seabirds visit the Pribilof Islands, 800 miles (1,280 km) from Anchorage.

Kitiwakes are cliff nesters. This colony is in Prince William Sound in Alaska.

California offers miles of coastline that are home to pelagic species and attract hundreds of migratory birds. Observers in Point Reyes National Seashore have tallied more than two hundred species in one day. The southern California and Arizona deserts include the Salton Sea, a desert sinkhole in the Colorado River that attracts migratory and wintering water birds. Another desert oasis, Big Morongo Preserve, attracts migrating birds of many species.

Texas is home to more than three hundred migratory and resident species. The Big Thicket National Preserve is noted for its diversity of habitats. Endangered whooping cranes make the Aransas National Wildlife Refuge their home from October through May.

Several Mexican species can be observed in the Rio Grande Valley, and more than three hundred species have been recorded in the Santa Ana National Wildlife Refuge.

Florida hotspots include Everglades National Park, consisting of more than one million acres. Southern Florida offers tropical habitats and many exotic species.

New Jersey's Cape May, at the southern-most tip of the Garden State, is one of the best birding hotspots in the country. It is a natural resting place for migrants heading across the bay, and is also noted for autumn raptor migrations.

Pennsylvania's Hawk Mountain, once a place where gunners went in the fall to shoot migrating hawks, is now a sanctuary and probably the most famous hotspot for raptors. More than 10,000 birds have been counted in one day.

A Great Egret (Casmerodius albus) *rookery draped with Spanish Moss. These herons often nest in colonies ranging from ten to thousands of individuals.*

Australia

Victoria's Rotamah Island boasts an observatory where emus (and kangaroos) graze, and a large number of water birds may be found. Coastal woodland, sand dunes, heath, and swamps provide a variety of bird habitats.

The Great Australian Bight in Western Australia is home to the Eyre Bird Observatory, where bush birds and shorebirds abound. Look for malleefowl and honeyeaters.

Barren Grounds Observatory in New South Wales is situated on a plateau overlooking the Illawarra coastline. The Nature Reserve was originally set up to protect the endangered Ground Parrot, Eastern Bristlebird, and Long-nosed Potoroo. Heath, woodland, and rainforest ensure a diversity of birds.

In the breeding season, Gannets (Sula bassanus) gather in large coastal colonies like this one in Ile Bonaventure, Quebec. In winter, the birds live at sea but can often be seen near the shore.

At Broome, Western Australia, waders such as Redshanks, Broadbilled Sandpipers, Asian Dowitchers, and Yellow Wagtails may be seen, among the more than 230 other species of birds that frequent the area.

Other Australian hotspots include the Great Barrier Reef, the Atherton Tablelands, Lord Howe Island, Lawn Hill National Park, and Kakadu National Park.

England and Europe

In England, the Royal Society for the Protection of Birds maintains over 100 wildlife reserves. A list can be obtained by contacting the RSPB at the address given at the back of the book.

Some spots to consider include Adur Estuary, West Sussex; Berney Marshes, Norfolk; Campfield Marsh, Cumbria; Coquet Island, Northumberland; Elmley Marshes, Kent; Frampton Marshes, Lincolnshire; Havergate Island, Suffolk; Langstone Harbour, Hampshire; Morecambe Bay, Lancashire; Ouse Washes, Cambridgeshire; Rye House Marsh, Hertfordshire; Lake Vyrnwy, Powys, Wales; Grassholm, Dyfed, Wales; KenDee Marshes, Dumfries, Scotland; the Orkney Islands, Scotland; and Rathlin Island, Antrim, Northern Ireland, are all good for seeing shorebirds.

Other areas include Arne, Dorset, Aylesbeare Common, Devon; Church Wood, Buckinghamshire; Church Wood, Blean, Kent;

Churnet Valley Woods, Staffordshire; Dungeness, Kent; Eastwood, Manchester; Fore Wood, East Sussex; Fowlmere, Cambridge; Garston Wood, Dorset; Geltsdale, Cumbria; Highnam Woods, Gloucester; Leighton Moss, Lancashire; The Lodge, Bedfordshire; Minsmere, Suffolk; Nagshead, Gloucestershire; Northward Hill, Kent; Wolves Wood, Suffolk; Dyffryn Wood, Powys, Wales; Gwynedd, Wales; Lochwinnoch, Strathclyde, Scotland; Dumfries, Scotland.

In Europe, The Camargue in France is known for its flamingos and waterbird populations. The Caspian Sea, between Europe and Asia; the straits of Gibraltar, between Spain and Africa; and the Bosphorous in Turkey are also known for diverse populations of birds. The Coto D'Oñana in Spain is a wetlands where Spanish Imperial Eagles may be seen.

Birding hotspots all over the world may be found by contacting local birdwatching societies, which can direct you further.

Canada

Ontario's Point Pelée National Park, a strip of land about 9 miles (14 km) long that extends into Lake Erie, is one of the most famous birding hotspots in the world. May is the best month, when warblers, tanagers, thrushes, grosbeaks, swallows, raptors, herons, shorebirds, and more congregate on the strip to rest before crossing the lake.

Québec's Gaspé Peninsula is the place to see pelagic species. Gannets, common murres, puffins, and razorbills are among the thousands of pelagic birds to be found on Bonaventure Island, just off the coast.

Nova Scotia's Cape Breton Highlands National Park and the Bay of Fundy are famous for the large numbers of migrating shorebirds that congregate there. Nova Scotia is also one of the major nesting areas for Bald Eagles.

Because they provide so many varied habitats, "edges" such as the ecozones between water, open fields, and woods are especially rich areas for birds.

FINDING BIRDS IN DIFFERENT HABITATS

Woodlands   Woodlands of all kinds provide birds with a wide array of microhabitats to exploit. As the term implies, a microhabitat is a small portion of a habitat. For example, the largest American woodpecker, the Pileated Woodpecker, ranges from southern Canada south through Florida and the Gulf states. It shares most of its range with the White-breasted Nuthatch, and both share the microhabitat that could be called "tree trunks." But a closer look at the habits of these two species shows that they use their common microhabitat in different ways. In typical woodpecker fashion, the Pileated Woodpecker excavates holes in large, mature trees. It has a barbed tongue that it inserts into holes to harpoon grubs hiding there. The tongues of woodpeckers are highly specialized. In addition to being barbed, so that an impaled, wriggling, wormlike grub cannot escape once it is stabbed, woodpecker tongues are also extremely long, flexible, and strong. They wrap around the back of a woodpecker's skull and attach just above the bird's eyes.

While Pileated Woodpeckers are drilling large holes in the trunks of mature trees and harpooning hidden insects, White-breasted Nuthatches are spiraling headfirst down the trunk, gleaning insects from behind curls of bark. Even though the two birds (as well as many others, such as Downy Woodpeckers, Hairy Woodpeckers, Yellow-bellied Sapsuckers, Red-bellied Woodpeckers, Brown Creepers, and Black-and-White Warblers) share the same microhabitat, each has an exclusive hunting territory. It seems to be a general rule that each species uses the microhabitat in a unique way, thus avoiding competition for the same resources.

Microhabitat is one component of a species' ecological niche or role in the environment. Thus, we would speak of the White-breasted Nuthatch as filling the role of "feathered tree cleaner." To further define its ecological niche, we might say that it is an "insect hunter that

Red-Bellied Woodpeckers (Nekaberoes carikubys) *are specialized for tree-trunk living. They hammer out the larvae of wood boring insects, carve out cavities for nesting, and use drumming and tapping to communicate.*

searches trunks and branches, moving from the top to the base of a tree trunk." Because bird species specialize to share habitats and microhabitats, more species can live together. This phenomenon is called species packing and it reaches its apex in tropical woodlands, where the stable climate has allowed species to adapt to narrower and narrower ranges of food choices and nesting sites.

Finding Birds in Woodlands

Whether you are birding in the woods in your hometown or the woods outside of Bombay, song is the key to finding birds in woodlands, especially where vegetation is dense. As previously mentioned, average birders hear more birds than they see and the rewards of learning birdcalls cannot be minimized. When you do hear a bird, keep still and listen. Try to identify the call; try to create a mnemonic device that will help you remember it. Then locate the bird. Some birds are remarkable ventriloquists, difficult to see even though they sing quite loudly. It often helps to have several people listen and then slowly point in the direction from which the call seems to be coming.

When you visit any woodland, remember that different species use the habitat in different ways. While woodpeckers, creepers, nuthatches, and treecreepers are typically found on tree trunks, others, like thornbirds, thrashers, scrubwrens, quail-thrushes, and ovenbirds, are ground-dwellers that seldom perch in branches. Some flit through thick undergrowth and others rarely come down from the sunlit canopy. Many, like babblers, are found in more than one of these zones.

Dawn and dusk are the best times to find birds in woodlands. It is then that males sing to audibly renew the limits of their territories. Except for nocturnal birds, the majority are most active and therefore most conspicuous in the early morning hours. Diurnal birds (those that are active during the daylight hours) tend to drowse and digest their food at midday. A second peak of activity occurs at or just before dusk. Try to time your birding to include either dawn or dusk.

An Oriole perched on a leafy limb is a welcome sight to birdwatchers scanning the treetops.

Tips for Woodland Birding

Whether you are visiting a tropical rainforest or a temperate deciduous forest, watch for movement and listen for birdcalls. Watch for food sources: Flowering or fruiting trees will attract a host of birds; hatching insects or an exodus of winged ants or termites will bring insectivorous birds. Ecotones, or edges between habitats—where a woodland meets a meadow, for example—are often most productive for birders because they attract species characteristic of each habitat. Edges of woodland ponds and streams are similarly productive. If you visit a tropical rainforest wear a red T-shirt and sit (but not directly on the ground) in a sunlit opening in the forest. Your red shirt should attract hummingbirds that will hover before your eyes, trying to determine if you are a giant flower. Because warblers utilize every layer of a forest, warbler hotspots tend to be open woodlands with plenty of undergrowth, protection from wind and available fresh water.

Wetlands   The word "wetlands" implies flooded ground. It is a catchall term that includes salt marshes, fresh water marshes, swamps, bogs, and creek and river bottoms. Some of these feature expanses of open sky over reeds or cattails; others have dense, shrubby underbrush. Because of their rich array of foods, wetlands teem with birds and are among the best places to go birdwatching. Microhabitats of wetland birds are highly variable. Herons spear their prey, osprey plunge for fish, ducks dabble for aquatic invertebrates and plants, swallows and swifts seine aerial plankton with their facial bristles, flycatchers "hawk" at passing dragonflies, vireos call from hidden nests.

Finding Birds in Wetlands

Wetlands teach you to scan with binoculars. Find a place with some elevation: an observation platform or a high bank. In open areas the lazy birder will stand in an open car door with elbows propped on the car's roof top. To scan, methodically and slowly sweep the horizon, moving from left to right and back again, watching for movement. When you see something flying, follow it with your binoculars until you can see its field marks. Because open wetlands typically have vast expanses of reeds and saltmarsh grasses, you will quickly learn how useful a spotting 'scope can be. If you don't own one, ask birders that you meet in the field if they would let you look through their 'scopes for a few moments. Most birders are more than happy to share their equipment.

Swampy places are the opposite extreme. In a flooded woodland you will need to move as silently as possible. In such an environment, listening for calls becomes extremely important.

Some of the most exciting birding can be done from a canoe or motorboat with a small, quiet engine. In the early spring, before mosquitoes become pestiferous, freshwater swamps can be fascinating places. A canoe will allow you to sneak up on many birds ordinarily too shy to allow humans to approach but less frightened of humans in canoes. A canoe trip that includes either dawn or dusk birding will allow you close-up visions of birds that are otherwise out of range.

Streams and creeks, ponds, and lakes may offer you a seated vantage point where you can watch activity at the ecotone between woodland or grassland and water. As with woodland birding, ecotones that include water offer excellent opportunities to see more species of birds.

Tips for Wetland Birding

Insects may be a problem in late spring and early summer, so be prepared with long-sleeved shirt, long pants, and insect repellent. In the far north, a hat with a veil that covers your neck may be a useful investment. In areas where ticks are a problem, dress to fool them. Wear long socks and tuck your trousers inside. Wear long sleeves, and tuck your shirt into your pants. If you follow this plan and wear light-colored clothing, you will spot most ticks on your clothing and be able to remove and kill them before they are able to reach your skin. To further protect yourself, apply insect repellent that has a high percentage of DEET (the active ingredient in insect repellents) to your clothing, being careful not to get any on your skin. Finally, don't sit on the ground.

A fog-shrouded flock of feeding Mallards (Anas platyrhinos) gives many opportunities for behavior-watching.

Take along a poncho or find a convenient rock where you will not give chiggers and related pests the opportunity to climb aboard.

In wetland birding, as in woodland birding, try to position yourself so that the sun is shining on the scene, not in your eyes. If you look into the sun, all details of color and plumage will fade into a black silhouette.

Wilson's Plovers (Steganopus tricolor) are unusual in feeding both day and night on small crustaceans, shoreline insects, crabs, and sand worms.

Study your field guide before going to an open wetland or a beach. In these areas, voice is of much less importance than visual identification, and you will need to know the field marks of ducks, geese, swans, and other waterfowl. Depending on the season, also study swallows, gulls, terns, and other shorebirds. Try to learn the silhouettes of different waterfowl and study the pictures of the birds flying as well as those floating on the water. A 'scope is often essential when birding in saltmarshes and on beaches.

Wetlands are often the best places to see hawks and owls. To see owls hunting, arrive shortly before dusk and position yourself so that you can survey an expanse of marsh or other wetland. Begin to scan the scene, watching for movement. Be patient and you may be rewarded with the sight of an owl flying low over the grasses. Also scan the ecotone between trees and marsh. Owls often fly to perches in these areas before launching off for a night's hunting.

City Birding Cities are interesting places for birding, mainly because surprising species appear. Not only do most large cities have parks with respectable breeding populations of birds, but the unnatural environment allows certain introduced alien species to thrive, and in many case, outcompete natives. European Starlings, House Sparrows, House Finches, and Rock Doves are common in many large cities. Pet birds and shipments of exotic birds meant for the pet trade occasionally escape from airports, leading to colonies of Monk Parakeets, Budgerigars, Canary-Winged Parakeets, and Nanday Conures in Miami and New York City. It is also not uncommon to hear and see other parrots, cockatiels, and even Scarlet Macaws in city neighborhoods. Once you learn to recognize the calls of parrots, you will begin to hear them from time to time in and around city parks, or even on city streets. Last spring and summer I watched the antics of a very vocal pale blue parakeet that lived in the supports of a streetlight just outside my living room window in the city. It seemed to be healthy and fed like a pigeon on crusts of pizza and ends of sandwiches that people had thrown into the gutter. Then one day the bird was gone. I also remember an escaped Scarlet Macaw that sat in the leafless branches of a London Plane Tree on a busy corner in New York City's Greenwich Village. A small crowd gathered and watched as maintenance crews from New York University tried to capture the

A Peregrine Falcon (Falco peregrinus) *at home amongst the skyscrapers in downtown Denver, Colorado.*

bird but only succeeded in frightening it to higher branches. Eventually a man in a suede baseball jacket appeared, nimbly climbed the tree, and with a few, sure movements cradled the big, gaudy bird in one arm as he climbed down. If he wasn't the bird's owner, he was certainly someone accustomed to handling large parrots.

Large populations of pigeons and House sparrows provide a rich source of food for Peregrine Falcons and Kestrels, who also adapt themselves to city life, breeding on rooftops and skyscraper ledges. The "killy-killy-killy" call of Kestrels is commonly heard in New York City, but few non-birders are aware that breeding falcons are about. While Kestrels are rather anonymous and relatively invisible to nonbirders, Peregrine Falcons are much more apparent. You may notice the messy banners and splashes of "whitewash" (a polite term for the viscous excrement characteristic of raptors) down the sides of buildings or on the street.

Finding Birds in Cities

Parks, zoos, and rooftops are all logical places to look for birds. Backyard gardens also offer refuges, but because most of these can't be seen from city streets, you'll have to listen carefully. Try to develop the skill of always listening for birds and you will be surprised at what you hear. One of the best times to hear birds is early in the morning, when the city noises are at their quietest. There is a dawn chorus of birds in the city, too. It isn't as rich and wild-sounding as that heard in Australia's Outback, but it has its charms.

Tips for City Birding

City parks are often excellent places to watch migrants. For some reason, perhaps because of the exertions of migration or perhaps because they are slightly disoriented, migrants are occasionally less shy in city parks and in suburban gardens and streets than they are in their natural environments. Backyards, tree-lined streets, and even vest-pocket parks are home to many birds. Tucking a pair of mini-binoculars into your pocket will allow you to observe city birds. You'll be surprised at what you will see.

Other Places to Try

• Airports, especially small ones where you can see much of the runway from service roads, often have interesting birds visiting them.

• Dumps. You can learn a great deal about gull behavior while watching them joust over newly opened trash bags. If you travel, form the habit of visiting landfills and dumps to see the species that make use of these rich, if unsavory resources.

• Sewage ponds. You can see a great variety of shorebirds in these shallow ponds where treated wastewater settles. They're feeding on aquatic invertebrates.

• Abandoned buildings. Look for pellets that give away the presence of roosting owls.

Canada Geese (Branta canadensis) *settle in many city parks such as this one in Vancouver, British Columbia, Canada.*

• Roadsides. As you drive, watch for birds perched on roadsides. Many hawks, vultures, and ravens commonly are seen at roadsides. Some are hunting small animals in short grass, others are smelling or watching for carrion.

• Silhouette Watching. Often, while you are driving you will catch a glimpse of a bird that flies overhead for a moment before disappearing. Study the silhouettes in your field guide to help you identify these birds. Also watch for characteristic patterns of flight and wing postures.

FEEDING BIRDS

No one knows for certain where the practice of feeding wild birds originated. The earliest written records concerning birds are dated around 3,000 B.C. and suggest that primitive people kept track of the arrivals and departures of different species. The appearance of particular species helped mark the seasons and indicated when it was time for planting and harvesting.

Often, the appearance of a bird was regarded as an omen, and one theory on the origins of feeding birds suggests that primitive people may have offered food to draw the omen-birds to them. Today, people all over the world continue the practice of attracting birds by maintaining feeders.

Novice birdwatchers may find it easier to establish a feeding station and observe the birds that use it than to locate birds in the field. Feeder birds return to the same station again and again, giving ample time to observe the appearance and behavior of each individual.

Establishing a feeder does not have to be an expensive affair, though you can certainly spend a bundle on fancy equipment and commercial seed mixes. The location of your feeder and the type of seeds that fill it are far more important considerations than the appearance or cost of the feeder itself.

There are literally hundreds of feeder designs to choose from, but the one favored by many birders is the hopper. A covered holding bin is filled from the top of the feeder, and the seed filters down into a feeding tray as the birds eat. Hopper feeders may be hung or mounted on a pole.

One disadvantage of hopper feeders, or any type of tray feeder, is that bird feces can come into contact with it and contaminate the seed. Cleaning the feeder regularly eliminates the danger of spreading disease.

Feeders provide welcome dietary supplementation—especially when snow covers wild food sources, making them inaccessible to birds.

Finches, siskins, and redpolls are attracted to tube or cylinder feeders filled with black thistle, or Niger seeds. Although feces cannot contaminate the seed in a tube feeder, tube feeders are more susceptible to mildew. Again, proper maintenance will eliminate potential problems.

Window feeders range from clear plastic bubbles that attach directly to the windowpane with suction cups to greenhouse-type feeders that fit in the window frame and extend into the house. One-way coating on the glass prevents the birds from becoming frightened but allows close-up viewing in the comfort of home.

Coated-wire feeders are available for holding slabs of beef suet, but you can also use mesh bags, gourds, and halved coconut shells. In any case, expect to lose at least a few suet feeders to raccoon bandits.

You will attract greater variety of species by establishing more than one feeding station at different levels. For example, seed scattered directly on the ground attracts sparrows, towhees, juncos, doves, and other ground-feeding species. Feeders placed a few feet above the ground will attract grosbeaks, cardinals, chickadees, titmice, and other species that normally feed at that elevation.

Locate your feeders in areas that provide numerous perches and nearby shelter—trees or shrubbery where birds can take cover when the neighbor's cat breezes through the yard.

Food Favorites   Commercially packaged birdseed is readily available and may seem inexpensive compared to bulk seed, but it does not always contain the most suitable mixtures and very often much of the seed is wasted.

Feeding birds has become something of an art in itself, and a multitude of seeds are available for birders to concoct their own mixes. One way to determine which foods are favored by the birds in your area is to ask the birds. Select two or three days where clear weather is promised (so you won't need a covered feeder) and set out one tray for each type of seed you wish to testmarket (pie plates work well). Place about a cupful of seed in each tray. By keeping an eye on the rate of disappearance of each type, you'll soon know your birds' preferences.

The following have been established as the standard favorites of most feeder birds:

• Sunflower. The all-time favorite of many species. Sunflower seeds are available in three varieties: Perdovic, a small, black oil seed; black and white striped seed; and gray and white striped seed. Sunflower seed is preferred by many finches, chickadees, grosbeaks, cardinals, jays, titmice, and sparrows.

• Thistle. Also known as Niger, thistle is imported from Africa and is comparatively expensive but never wasted. It is favored by finches, redpolls, siskins, chickadees, juncos, sparrows, towhees, doves, and more.

Painted Buntings (Passerina ciris) are colorful visitors to feeders in Florida and the southeastern United States to Texas.

• Millet. Millet is available in several varieties; the preferred is white millet.

• Corn. Finely cracked corn is probably the best choice; the small size enables a greater variety of species to feed. Whole kernel corn can be offered in a separate feeder for blackbirds, doves, and other larger species—even squirrels. Whole kernel corn spread on the ground will also attract pheasants and grouse.

• Peanuts. Relatively expensive, but appreciated! Shelled, cracked peanuts are preferred by small birds to whole peanuts, which can be placed in a separate feeder to accommodate the larger, more aggressive species.

Small birds like the American Goldfinch (Carduelis tristis), *the Pine Siskin* (Carduelis pinus) *and the House Finch* (Carpodacus mexicanus) *are common visitors at bird feeders in most of North America.*

Additional Foods   Numerous foods that birds will readily eat can be used to supplement the more conventional foods

• Fruit. Fresh, thawed, or reconstituted dried fruits offered in summer feeders attract orioles, tanagers, thrushes, some warblers, and other species you don't normally expect to visit a feeder. Fruit can also be offered in winter feeders. Some suggestions are bananas, apples, orange halves, any type of berries, grapes and cherries, and melon pieces. Try putting out a spoonful of fruit jam or jelly.

• Eggs. Scrambled eggs are best. Save the shells, wash and crush, and place of feeders as an additional source of minerals.

• Mealworms. Mealworms can be purchased in pet shops, or you can raise your own in a container of dry rolled oats. Mealworms are the larvae of the flour beetle and are eaten by many species of birds. Offer in a walled tray to prevent escape.

• Baked Goods. Stale bread, muffins, piecrusts, and the like can be crumbled and placed on the ground near feeders.

• Dog Food. Soak dry dog food in water until soft. Rehabilitators raise orphaned birds on dog food diets; it provides birds with the proper nutrients. Keeping a bag of dog food on hand is good insurance against an empty feeder in case you run out of seeds.

Feeder Maintenance   One of the most important aspects of feeding birds is maintaining a clean and healthy feeding environment. Feeders create crowded conditions that would not exist under natural circumstances. As mentioned, tray feeders allow birds to stand in the food, and feces will soon accumulate in the tray. Salmonellosis is a bacterial disease spread through contact with infected feces and is deadly to birds.

Regular cleaning, at least once a week and more in warm weather, will prevent the buildup of feces in tray feeders. In addition to cleaning the feeder itself, the accumulation of feces and discarded seed should be removed from the ground beneath feeders.

Warm weather feeding is acceptable, but feeder maintenance during summer months is of utmost importance. Heat, humidity, spoiled seeds, and accumulated feces are a deadly combination. Tube feeders should be checked frequently to guard against mold and mildew from excessive heat and humidity.

This feeder, fillled with sunflower seeds, is equipped with a baffle designed to prevent squirrels from stealing seed.

Feeder Freeloaders   Face it. If you feed birds, you're going to feed squirrels, too. And possibly chipmunks, raccoons, and opossums, plus a variety of other four-legged creatures.

Most commercially available squirrel-proof feeders don't work. Of the ones that do, probably the best is called a Squirrel Spooker Pole, which has a sleeve that slides down the pole when the squirrel attempts to climb. The counterweighted sleeves slides back up the pole when the squirrel jumps off.

Repellents, poisons of any type, and grease, sometimes touted as effective squirrel-proof systems, should never be used, as they can harm or kill birds and other wildlife in the process.

Live-trapping any "pest" and releasing it elsewhere may solve the problem temporarily. Chances are another squirrel or raccoon will move into the territory where you have conveniently created a vacancy.

You may find it easier to admit defeat and feed the squirrels, too, using whole kernel corn, unshelled peanuts, leftover baked goods, and other relatively inexpensive foods in a separate feeder.

Most land birds prefer shallow water—a birdbath that slopes gently to a maximum depth of two to three inches (5.2 to 7.7cm) is best.

Birdbaths   Birds require fresh water throughout the year, for bathing as well as drinking, and are easily attracted to birdbaths placed near the feeding stations. This is especially true if fresh water is available during winter months, when normal sources of water may be frozen.

Thermostatically controlled heaters, available at farm supply stores or by mail order, will keep the water thawed. Water in motion is always more attractive to birds. During summer months a container leaking water one drop at a time, and suspended over the birdbath, will provide enough motion to entice a multitude of birds.

CHAPTER 5

Birds and Humans

*I*n the 1800s, crews of coal miners would descend into mine shafts equipped with pickaxes, lunch boxes, headlamps—and a caged bird. In subterranean passages that might be filled with deadly but imperceptible gases, a canary or other small songbird served the miners as a feathered gas detector. If the bird fell unconscious, they knew that something was wrong: The air in the mine wasn't safe to breathe. The miners could scramble to safety before they keeled over, too.

Similarly, declining bird populations today are sending us urgent messages about the health of our planet. Birds suffer from the effects of toxic substances like pesticides and PCBs. They succumb to poisons accidentally and carelessly introduced by sportsmen and industry. They get tangled in the refuse of our throwaway culture. In suburban backyards birds are relentlessly pursued by pampered predators that spend much of their nonhunting hours asleep on top of the television set. Despite their lethal effects on many birds, these are nevertheless small environmental problems, with relatively easy, painless solutions. Much more serious are the interconnected, and potentially disastrous, problems of climatic change caused by global warming, the effect of increased solar radiation on the world's food chains, the elimination of suitable habitat through tropical deforestation, the loss of wetlands, and urban encroachment. Each of these problems is exacerbated by the unprecedented explosion of the human population. As well, all of these problems—and their solutions—are global in scope. Unless we radically revise our values, the future of wild bird populations of many bird species—indeed, the future of all nature as we know it—is dim.

EASY FIXES

Some of the threats to Earth's bird populations can be dealt with relatively simply, and without great expense. These include chemical poisoning and predation by domestic animals.

DDT Poisoning   In Chapter 2, we discussed eggshell-thinning and the near-extinction of raptors, or large birds of prey like ospreys, hawks, and eagles, caused by the spraying of DDT to kill insects. We mentioned that predators receive all the DDT in all the food eaten by all the animals in a food chain because DDT is stored in fatty tissues instead of being eliminated. For example, a typical osprey food chain goes like this:

BACTERIA

MICROSCOPIC, SINGLE-CELLED ORGANISM

SMALL CRUSTACEAN
(barely visible to the naked eye)

MINNOW

LARGER FISH

OSPREY

To understand the impact of DDT, DDD, and DDE (the latter are two equally dangerous compounds into which DDT transforms), consider that the animal at each higher level of the food chain receives all the DDT stored in the

Illegally dumped hazardous wastes inevitably leach into the water table and thus enter the food chain. Like DDT, some of these toxic substances are susceptible to biological magnification.

fat-containing compounds of each meal. DDT is insoluble in water, but tends to coat organic matter that it encounters.

Finally, consider that in the course of a day, an osprey catches several fish, consuming and storing all the DDT, DDD, and DDE in the flesh of each fish. When you imagine ospreys plunging out of the sky to catch and eat contaminated fish every day of their lives, the magnitude of poisoning becomes even clearer.

Ospreys are not the only birds that are affected by eggshell-thinning. Virtually all raptors and shorebirds suffer from the problem. To make matters worse, DDT has a long life. It takes decades for each molecule to degrade into a harmless compound. And, because of the global circulation of air and water, DDT doesn't stay where it is sprayed. Antarctic penguins and arctic auks have DDT in their fat deposits, although DDT has never been used there for pest control.

When it was developed, DDT was thought to be a miracle pesticide because it was effective and longlasting. Its negative effects unknown, it was widely sprayed to kill agricultural and garden pests, battle houseflies and roaches in homes, and kill malarial mosquitoes in swamps. In the United States, the use of DDT reached a peak in 1959, and bird populations declined correspondingly. Not all birds are as resistant to DDT as raptors and shorebirds. High doses will short-circuit a small bird's nervous system, causing convulsions and death. After aerial spraying, largely to kill agricultural pests, windrows of dead birds were common.

In 1962, Rachel Carson, a marine biologist whose books about the sea, *The Sea Around Us* and *Under the Sea Wind*, had earned her literary fame, wrote *Silent Spring* to protest the use of DDT. Her work shocked and alerted the public to the dangers of continued use of pesticides. With much kicking and screaming from the industries threatened with loss of profits, DDT and other chlorinated hydrocarbon pesticides began to be phased out in 1969. They were

The problem with aerial spraying of pesticides is that these chemicals don't stay put. They volatize in the atmosphere and get blown far from the crop fields where they were meant to combat pests.

eventually banned, except for use in dire emergencies, in the United States in 1971. Most European nations and Australia also banned chlorinated hydrocarbon pesticides (DDT, aldrin, dieldrin, heptachlor), but corporations still sell these longlasting pesticides in nearly all the countries of Central and South America, in Africa, and in Asia.

The banning of DDT alone was not sufficient to bring back populations of raptors that had fallen dangerously low. Captive breeding programs were aimed at the eventual release and reintroduction of the Peregrine Falcon. In the Eastern United States, eggs with normal shells were transplanted from nests of southern Ospreys to nests of northern ospreys that could only produce fragile-shelled eggs. Through the efforts of osprey researchers, populations of these fish hawks are climbing to healthy levels.

Penguins such as these Adelies (Pygoscelis adelie) have DDT in their fat reserves, even though they live far from places where DDT has been sprayed.

To date, our response to the dangers of pesticides has been heartening. It forms one of the few bright spots in the otherwise dismal story of the relationship between birds and man. It shows that we can and will change our habits to protect the fragile environment, as long as suitable substitutes are found for products that are dangerous.

Lead Poisoning of Waterfowl   The average hunter is only an average marksman, discharging between five and thirty shotgun shells for every bird felled. Each shotgun shell is filled with about 250 lead pellets that pepper lake bottoms and waterways. Imagine all those gunners blazing away in all the marshes and duck blinds in the flyways of the world and you begin to appreciate the magnitude of the problem.

Ducks and geese commonly eat the spent pellets along with grit and seeds; the pellets are pulverized in the gizzard and the lead enters the bird's circulation. Lead poisoning affects brain function and interferes with the normal production of hemoglobin; a single pulverized lead pellet is fatal to most ducks, geese, and other water-fowl. Each year millions of waterfowl die from lead poisoning; it is a major factor contributing to the current, somewhat mysterious decline in waterfowl populations. Although there are some thoughtless, diehard hunters who refuse to change from lead to stainless steel shot, most hunters realize that its continued use will ultimately end their sport and have stopped using lead. It will take time for all those pellets to be safely buried in deep sediments, out of the reach of dabbling waterfowl. Until then, lead poisoning will continue to be a problem.

To reduce lead poisoning, it is now law that all waterfowl hunters use shells with stainless steel shot rather than lead pellets.

Bell the Cat   Two years ago, researchers in Britain intensively studied a village in Bedfordshire, to determine the extent of predation by house cats. For a year, cat owners (45 percent of villagers, about equivalent to the British national average) were asked to bag the remains of any animals that their cats brought home; the bags were collected weekly and the catch identified. The results of this study were surprising. Cats were found to be opportunistic predators, taking whatever prey was most plentiful. Small mammals (mice, voles, shrews, rabbits, and others) made up 65 percent of the cats' kill; small birds (sparrows, thrushes, blackbirds, robins, and others) made up the remaining 35 percent. The interesting thing is that all of these cats were well fed by their owners! The amount of feeding did not seem to affect the hunting proclivities of these house cats; they continued to be ruthless killers even though hunger did not force them to hunt.

A follow-up study by these same researchers investigated the effect of house cat predation on the local population of House Sparrows. They determined that between 33 and 50 percent of all deaths of House Sparrows were due to cats. Extrapolating these local figures to a national scale, we see that about seventy million animals are killed annually by well-fed house cats; at least twenty million of them are birds.

The instinctive play and stalk behavior of cats makes them curious and endearing as kittens. As adults, though, cats are relentless bird killers.

Unfortunately, these may be minimal figures. A similar American study found that cats brought home only half of their total catch. They often either abandoned their kills or ate them in the field. This information should drastically alter our view of pet cats, which enjoy a current popularity that rivals that of man's best friend. At the least, the conscientious cat owner will put a bell on his or her cat before letting it out to stalk the already stressed local wildlife.

PCBs   Polychlorinated biphenyls are industrial chemicals that up until 1977 were used in insulating materials for electric capacitors and transformers, in hydraulic fluids, and in the manufacture of some plastics. If PCBs are not disposed of carefully, they can enter the environment and seriously affect food chains, especially those in lakes and oceans. Just like DDT and other chlorinated hydrocarbons, PCBs bioaccumulate in the tissues of top carnivores. PCBs that are burned vaporize and condense on dust particles that settle onto waters or environmental surfaces. Eventually they are washed into aquatic ecosystems. Leakage from industrial waste disposal sites is a continual problem. In birds, especially fish-eating birds like terns, PCBs cause tumors and improper growth of embryos.

Although a staggering amount of PCB is currently in use all over the world and PCBs will continue to wash into aquatic and marine waters, the problem has a relatively easy solution. Due to their extreme toxicity to human beings and wildlife, PCBs are presently being phased out of use in industry. In time they will cease to interfere with wild bird populations.

Introduced Alien Species   In the 1890s there was a movement on the part of certain anglophiles to introduce into America all of the birds mentioned in the writings of Shakespeare. The United States and Canada owe the presence of House Sparrows and European Starlings to this effort. Originally, the starling occurred in most of Eurasia, ranging from the Mediterranean to Norway and east to Siberia. Although there were three earlier failed attempts to establish starlings in the United States, the successful introduction occurred in April 1890, when eighty birds were released into Central Park in New York City. Ten years later the starling was settled and breeding in the area and has since expanded its range westward across North America and south into Mexico. Starlings were also introduced into Australia, with similar results. Starlings are aggressive birds that compete with native birds and oust them from their nesting places.

Air pollution makes the air visible in Denver, Colorado. Greenhouse gases such as methane and carbon dioxide form a portion of this petrochemical smog.

The House Sparrow, really a Eurasian Weaver Finch, was introduced into the United States in the 1850s when eight pairs were released in Brooklyn, New York. In those horse-and-buggy days, the birds thrived on the spilled grain associated with horses and farms; they are now naturalized all over the United States. Like the starling, the English Sparrow negatively affects the numbers of native Eastern Bluebirds, House Wrens, Purple Martins, Tree Swallows, and Barn Swallows. Building bird houses specifically for these species may help them to compete.

Acid Rain   Acid rain is produced when sulfur or nitrogen oxides are dissolved in precipitation. Sulfur dioxide and nitrous oxides are by-products of burning fossil fuels. North American and European industry has been slow to adopt the emission control systems that could curb the output of these chemicals into the air; automobile manufacturers and drivers continue to ignore their contribution to the problem. As a result, although rain, snow, and other forms of precipitation normally have a pH or hydrogen-ion concentration between 6 and 7.6, many freshwater streams and lakes in western Europe, Scandinavia, and central and eastern North America have a pH between 4 and 5. Although acidification has been noted in Australian waters, the problem is not as severe.

Acid waters are strange, sterile places, devoid of the teeming mass of life that usually characterizes fresh waters. They lack normal populations of protozoans, microscopic worms, crustaceans, larval insects, amphibians at all stages of their life cycles, and fish of all sizes. Obviously, because acidified lakes offer no food, wading and fish-eating birds disappear from them.

This relationship is straightforward. If you cut off the food supply, you starve the population that feeds upon it. We are only now beginning to realize that acidified precipitation and acid waters have effects that are much more complicated and subtle than we once thought. Acid rain may be behind the mysterious declines in waterfowl populations that have been observed since the 1960s. Studies on Black Ducks are most comprehensive to date and, although the findings are only tentative, it may be that at critical periods in their lives these otherwise vegetarian ducks must feed on the animal protein available in normal, unacidified freshwaters. Researchers hypothesize that if ducklings or egg-producing adult females cannot find protein in the form of snails, worms, and small crustaceans, normal growth will not ensue. Ducklings raised in lifeless, acid waters died; ducklings grew and thrived in waters with neutral pH and rich populations of small, aquatic animals.

Shrinking Wetlands   Biologists often refer to "wetlands," and no one understands what they are talking about. Everyone knows what a swamp or a marsh is, but few people know what a wetland is. Let's be clear: Wetlands is a cryptic way of saying swamps, bogs, freshwater marshes, saltwater marshes, river edges, pond edges, partially flooded forests, potholes, or muskegs. It is a shorthand way to refer to a wide variety of habitats that feature standing bodies of water for all or part of the year.

Smoke stacks emit oxides of nitrogen and sulfur that mix with precipitation to brew acid rain, acid snow, and acid fog.

Biologists speak of wetlands with a kind of incandescent reverence, but few other people understand why. Developers see wetlands as lovely flat stretches of ground that are perfect for housing developments (once all that watery muck and ooze have been drained, of course). Developers love wetlands because once they are drained, wetlands become high-ticket real estate, close to prime property fronting on lakes or the ocean. Town planners see wetlands as perfect sites for landfills. The argument goes something like this: "No one wants to live on these mosquito-infested marshes. Might as well make good use of them. Put the new dump there." Farmers see wetlands as flat fields that, once they are drained, will be perfect for growing a variety of crops.

What we must do is convince people that wetlands are valuable in themselves because the biological health of a community rests on whether or not its marshy areas are intact. Far from being waste places, wetlands provide nursery areas for all sorts of animals from lobster larvae to muskrats to eagles. Birds need wetlands to nest, feed, and rest in during migration. Thus far, though, we haven't been able to make much of a dent in the natural tendency of developers to turn wetlands into tracts of bilevel houses and of town planners to fill them with refuse. Since 1900 the United States has lost 54 percent of its original wetland area, Britain has lost between 50 and 60 percent, and the entire world has lost approximately half of its wetland areas.

THE CENTRAL ECOLOGICAL PROBLEM: HARDER TO FIX

The overwhelming ecological problem facing humankind today is at once simple and baffling and very difficult to fix. Unlike DDT or PCBs or lead shot, the human population explosion cannot be legislated away. There are just too many people for our planet to support. In a very real sense, we are breeding ourselves out of existence. The burgeoning human population has a negative effect on the other ecological problems faced by birds, humans, and all of nature today. Loss of habitat, global warming, and increased radiation are all linked to this central ecological problem.

Loss of Habitat: Deforestation   In 1988 satellites surveying the world sent back disturbing images of how rapidly tropical forests were being cleared. In response, temperate zone ecologists began to sound the alarm, mainly because few tropical countries are rich enough to support satellite imaging programs. One of the issues that was generally ignored is that deforestation is a way of life in the temperate zone, too. The furor over deforestation of old growth forests of the northwestern United States, which focuses on loss of habitat for the Spotted Owl versus loss of jobs for loggers, highlights the desperation of an industry based on a vanishing resource. In the

Amazon, people are only now beginning to realize that they have been using outmoded, poorly conceived models for development. Like Don Quixote, they have been charging windmills, trying to apply American agricultural practices and modernization methods that simply do not work well in the tropics. The price, both north and south of the equator, has been the loss of forest habitat.

Recent estimates put the rate of destruction of tropical forests worldwide at 40 to 50 million acres (16–29 million ha) annually, or 80 acres (3.2 ha) per minute. Temperate losses are significantly less, but nevertheless, as the human population grows, temperate forests are eroded. As the forests are destroyed, animal and plant species also disappear, diminishing the variety of life on Earth. One current, conservative estimate is that the world's stock of plants and animals dwindles by 0.2 percent per year. This doesn't sound very significant. Two-tenths of one percent of your income probably won't buy very much, but consider: The species of plants that are disappearing are becoming extinct. To paraphrase American naturalist Charles William Beebe (1877–1967), a new heaven and a new Earth will have to pass away before their kind are seen again. So, the problem is very grave, indeed, and with every acre that is cleared, the planet becomes warmer.

Global Warming   Burning fossil fuels produce carbon dioxide gas and leads to an increase of carbon dioxide in the atmosphere. In what is somewhat erroneously called the greenhouse effect, the atmosphere gets warmer because carbon dioxide acts as a physical barrier that prevents heat from escaping. Carbon dioxide is not the only greenhouse gas: Methane is its partner in atmospheric heat-trapping. It is estimated that since the industrial revolution, when coal began to be burned to run factories and mills, there has been a 25 percent increase in carbon dioxide and a 100 percent increase in methane in the atmosphere. The extra heat that is trapped is equivalent to that produced by a small Christmas tree bulb burning in every square meter of the globe.

It is a fact that greenhouse gases have increased. We are certain of the effects of these gases. The controversy over global warming centers on questions of the intensity of the rise in temperature, how quickly it will happen, and the amount of devastation that will result. There is no doubt that global warming is presently underway—at this point, our attention should shift to finding ways to limit emissions of carbon dioxide and methane.

Automobiles are among the chief culprits in production of greenhouse gases. Each year an average American car pumps a ton of carbon dioxide into the atmosphere. Until there are atmosphere-friendly cars, everyone can try to drive less. Indeed, in California, this will soon be law.

Clear-cutting in the Northern Rockies, British Columbia, Canada.

No one is certain how much all those little Christmas tree lights burning in every square yard of the earth are going to heat up the atmosphere. The problem is too complex for even our most sophisticated computer models. What is certain is that human civilization has never known the planet to have an average warmth greater than 59°F (15°C)—until 1990, when the average global temperature reached 60°F (15.5°C). It is estimated that it will only take a 5°F to 7°F (3-4°C) rise to begin melting of the polar ice caps. The concomitant ecological upheavals would be particularly gruesome, ranging from flooding of coastlines to monstrously powerful hurricanes to massive disruptions of agriculture.

Most of these disaster scenarios recognize that natural habitats would be devastated by climatic changes of this magnitude. But most of us don't worry too much about birds in all of this. After all, we reason, they can fly. We think of birds as the epitome of freedom, creatures not bound to the earth, half belonging to the sky. What we fail to consider is the rigidity of the lives of most birds. Most are prisoners of their environments, beautifully adapted to a narrow range of choices as to habitat, food, and conditions for successful breeding. When global warming occurs, if humans have not acted to mollify its effects, birds will be further restricted. Without doubt, more species will vanish.

Increased Radiation   Like DDT and PCBs, chlorofluorocarbons (CFCs) are a human-made, technological breakthrough. They have proven so useful to industry that they have found their way into refrigeration, air-conditioning, aerosol sprays, insulation, health care, transportation, plastics, agriculture, fire fighting, telecommunications, and electronics. Annual emissions of CFCs approach a million tons; they are synonymous with modern standards of living.

CFCs are highly stable compounds. Once flushed out of an air conditioner, to use a common example, they slowly make their way to the upper atmosphere. The journey can take as long as five years. Once they reach a height of 6 to 30 miles (10 to 48 km) above the sur-

North America's largest acid rain emission site—Inco in Sudbury, Canada. This extremely tall smoke stack ejects oxides of nitrogen and sulfur high into the upper atmosphere.

face they encounter the ozone layer, a band of poisonous, unstable gas that absorbs lethal ultraviolet radiation coming from the sun. The ozone layer allows life to exist on the surface of the ground and in the upper levels of ocean. Without it, UV radiation makes its way to the surface where it damages and kills living cells. In humans, high doses of UV radiation cause skin cancer, blindness from cataracts, and severe damage to the immune system. UV radiation is also deadly to marine organisms, from plankton to marine algae and, indirectly, to marine birds and even to great whales. CFCs react with ozone, destroying the compound and thinning the ozone layer, allowing UV radiation to pass into the atmosphere.

In 1957, the British Antarctic Survey at Halley Bay began monitoring the stratosphere over Antarctica. In 1983, they reported that a huge hole had appeared in the ozone layer high above the South Pole. American researchers had received similar information from satellites several years earlier, but they disregarded the data, attributing it to "noise" in the system or computer bugs. No one could conceive that human activity had actually been able to change something as massive as the earth's atmosphere. But we have.

The hole in the ozone shield has been monitored continuously since the British team first brought it to the attention of the world. It is approximately the size of the United States of America. It appears in September and October when ozone is eroded by CFCs within cyclonic polar storms. The hole repairs itself and then reappears each year. In 1987 a similar hole developed over the North Pole. In 1988 it was estimated that stratospheric ozone levels in the Northern Hemisphere had decreased by 3 percent in the last twenty years.

Marine zooplankton and phytoplankton are severely threatened by the increased UV radiation that results from the loss of ozone. Phytoplankton not only reproduce less when exposed to UV radiation—many die. Like a collapsing house of cards, if phytoplankton are eliminated, whole marine food chains disappear. Zooplankton are tiny, sometimes microscopic animals that float in the oceans, feeding on bacteria and phytoplankton. They are particularly sensitive to UV radiation; most die within a few hours of exposure. Penguins, fish, squids, seals, and ultimately even the baleen whales depend upon zooplankton. And this is only a consideration of the most conspicuous animals found in Antarctica.

Human Reaction—The Montreal Protocol   In 1987 the Montreal Protocol, a global environmental agreement to control CFCs, was signed by sixty nations. In 1990 it was extended and strengthened to phase out CFCs within ten years. The signatory nations agreed to give financial and environmental assistance to developing countries to help them to progress without using CFCs. Although all nations of the world have not agreed to abide by its dictates, this is a truly historic agreement because it is global instead of national or regional in scope.

EFFECT ON BIRDS

All over the globe, bird populations are declining. The figures vary from country to country, but the trend is always the same: down. Although there are some happy reintroductions, such as the Capercaillie and Great Bustard in Britain and the Peregrine Falcon and Osprey in the United States, the story is repeated again and again: Numbers are declining. Fewer warblers are seen in the

If UV radiation continues to increase, fish kills at the margins of oceans will become all too common. And, as the marine food chain collapses, all other life on the planet will be negatively affected.

spring, fewer songbirds, ducks, geese, falcons, owls—the list goes on and on. There seem to be more starlings, cowbirds, and gulls, though, largely because they thrive in the habitats created by humans. We seem to have curbed the fascination with bird plumes that caused severe depletions of the birds of New Guinea in the 1880s and 1890s when fifty thousand skins were shipped out. Only twenty-five years later, the birds of paradise that had adorned women's hats had become rare. Perhaps we have learned something from the ruthless killing of Great Auks, Carolina Parakeets, Labrador Ducks, Passenger Pigeons, and Dodos that drove them to extinction.

Birds have long been objects of wonder and affection. The human fascination with the feathered aliens that share our planet runs deep. The current popularity of birding is only a modern manifestation of that age-old attraction. If only we can heed the warnings that the declines in bird populations are sending, perhaps we can scramble to safety, taking live, wild birds with us.

WHAT CAN YOU DO

Although the global ecological picture seems bleak, things can be improved, especially by informed, committed, conscientious citizens. Here are ten suggestions that will make a difference:

1. *Learn more.* Educate yourself by reading about ecology and about birds. Start with the references listed in the "Further Reading" section of this book and progress through those in your public library. To get up-to-date information, subscribe to one of the environmental magazines listed at the back of this book. Enroll in an ecology course in the adult education program of you high school, junior college, or nature museum. Watch the nature specials on public television.

2. *Think environmentally*. Remember that nothing happens in a vacuum; everything is inter-connected, so all of your actions have consequences in the environment. Recycle. Whenever possible, substitute walking or public transportation for driving your automobile. Try to cut down on short trips to neighborhood stores. Carpool whenever you can. Don't leave the lights burning unnecessarily. Try to use less energy and try to eat lower down on the food chain, i.e., more vegetables and fruits. Learn about Solar Box Cookers International. Try a solar cooker for yourself.

3. *Educate others*. Share your knowledge with your family and friends. Take children on nature walks. Teach them about birds, bugs, plants, and trees. Try to get out into the field at least once a month.

4. *Vote green*. Learn about local environmental issues and work to help candidates who are committed to them. Attend town meetings and show your support for the environment and conservation.

5. *Write letters*. Tell your elected representatives how you feel about bond issues, landfill choices, dump sites, and water management programs.

6. *Raise money*. Everyone can't be a wildlife biologist or field ornithologist, but everyone can contribute to their work. Join and give generous financial support to the Audubon Society, the Sierra Club, Rainforest Alliance, Solar Box Cookers International, Earth First, Greenpeace, or any of the conservation societies that do work you admire.

7. *Volunteer*. Local ornithological research programs need your help. Hawkwatchers, bird banding programs, Audubon Christmas Counts, and many other local projects need willing hands.

8. *Feed the birds*. Make your backyard into a nature sanctuary. Provide lots of cover as well as different kinds of food and water, In the spring, volunteer to help with bluebird trails and beach cleanups.

9. *Plant trees*.

10. *Find inspiration*. Read biographies of great naturalists and find role models to emulate, such as Margaret Morse Nice, Louise De Kiriline Lawrence, Edward A. Wilson, Alexander F. Skutch, Carl Akeley, Chico Mendes, and Jim Corbett.

Binocular Evaluation Checklist

Maker & Model No._____

Cost _____

Source_____

TYPE   Roof Prism?_____Porro Prism?_____   **SIZE**   Mini?_____Full-size?_____

QUICK OBSERVATIONS

	GOOD	BAD
POWER:	7x35	LESS
EXIT PUPIL:	5	LESS
WIDTH OF FIELD OF VIEW:	WIDE	NARROW
WEIGHT:	LIGHT	HEAVY
FEEL IN HANDS:	COMFY	HEAVY
FEEL AROUND NECK	LIGHT	HEAVY
EASE OF USE:	QUICK	CUMBERSOME

WIDE-ANGLE?_____

CENTER FOCUS?_____

ARMOR COAT?_____

HARD CASE?_____

LENS CAPS?_____

RAIN SHIELD?_____

STURDY STRAPS?_____

IN-STORE TESTING

COATED LENSES?_____

B MODEL?*_____

SINGLE FIELD OF VIEW?_____

IMAGE BRIGHTNESS

BRIGHT_____FAIRLY BRIGHT_____DIM_____

CLARITY OF IMAGE

CENTER_____ AROUND CLOCKFACE _____

SIMULTANEOUS‡_____

MANUFACTURER WARRANTY

RATING (1–22)

COMMENTS

Each "good" quality is worth one checkmark. Add checkmarks to evaluate binocs.

* Important if you wear, or ever plan to wear, eyeglasses.
‡ Edge and center clarity.

Field Guides

The following is a partial listing of the most readily available bird guides.

United States

Bull, J., E. Bull, G. Gold, and P.D. Prall. *Birds of North America Eastern Region*. New York: Macmillan Publishing, 1985.

Farrand, J. *Eastern Birds*. Chanticleer Press, New York: McGraw-Hill, 1988.

National Geographic Society. *Field Guide to the Birds of North America*, 2nd ed. 1987.

Peterson, R.T. *A Field Guide to the Birds East of the Rockies*. Boston: Houghton Mifflin, 1990.

Robbins, C.S., Bruun, and H.S. Zim. *A Guide to Field Identification: Birds of North America*. New York: Golden Press.

Canada

Godfrey, W. Earl. *The Birds of Canada*. Ottawa: National Museum of Canada Bulletin No. 203. Biological Series No. 73.

Peterson, R.T. *Field Guide to Western Birds*. Boston: Houghton Mifflin, 1990.

Further Reading

All bird books are not created equal; here are some of my favorites. Your local librarian should be able to help you locate some of the older titles.

On Becoming a Better Birder

Connor, Jack. *The Complete Birder: A Guide to Better Birding*. Boston: Houghton Mifflin, 1988.

Herman, Steven G. *The Naturalist's Field Journal: A Manual of Instruction Based on a System Established by Joseph Grinnell*. Vermillion, S.D.: Buteo Books, 1986.

Jellis, Rosemary. *Bird Sounds and Their Meaning*. Ithaca, N.Y.: Cornell University Press, 1977.

McElroy, Thomas P. *The Habitat Guide to Birding: A Guide to Birding East of the Rockies*. New York: Nick Lyons Books, 1974.

Specific Habitats or Special Groups of Birds

Knowler, Donald. *The Falconer of Central Park*. Toronto: Bantam Books, 1984.

Maslow, Jonathan Evan. *The Owl Papers*. New York: Vintage Books, 1983.

Mitchell, Andrew W. *The Enchanted Canopy: Secrets from the Rainforest Roof*. London: Fontana/Collins, 1986.

Phillips, John. *Dear Parrot: Pertaining to the Care, Nurture & Befriending of Man's Oldest Pet*. New York: Clarkson N. Potter, 1979.

Service, William. *Owl*. New York: Carroll & Graf Publishers, Inc., 1969.

Simpson, George Gaylord. *Penguins: Past and Present, Here and There*. New Haven, Conn.: Yale University Press, 1976.

Reference Books

Bent, Arthur Cleveland. *Life Histories of North American Birds*. New York: Dover Publications, Inc.

Berger, Andrew. *Bird Study*. New York: Dover Press reprint, 1971. Originally published in 1961 by John Wiley and Sons.

Ehrlich, Paul R., David S. Dobkin, and Darryl Wheye. *The Birder's Handbook*. New York: Simon & Schuster Inc., 1988.

Behavior Watching

Stokes, Donald W. *A Guide To Bird Behavior*, volumes 1–3.

History of Birding

Kastner, Joseph. *A World of Watchers: An Informal History of the American Passion for Birds*. San Francisco: Sierra Club Books, 1986.

Paleontology

Feduccia, Alan. *The Age of Birds*. Cambridge, Mass.: Harvard University Press, 1980.

Ecological Crisis

McKibben, Bill. *The End of Nature*. New York: Anchor Books/Doubleday, 1989.

Heroes

Akeley, Carl P. *In Brightest Africa*. New York: Doubleday, Page & Company, 1923.

Lawrence, Louise de Kiriline. *The Lovely and the Wild*. New York: McGraw-Hill, 1968.

Nice, Margaret Morse. *The Watcher at the Nest*. New York: MacMillan, 1939.

Skutch, Alexander F. *Birds Asleep*. Austin, Tex.: University of Texas Press, 1989.

Wilson, Edward A. *Diary of the Discovery Expedition to the Antarctic Regions 1901–1904*. Ed. by Ann Savours. London: Blanford Press.

On Birding in Canada

Burrows, Roger. *A Birdwatcher's Guide to Atlantic Canada: Vol. 1, Newfoundland and Labrador, Pelagic Ferries, and Offshore Islands.* St. John's, Newfoundland: Burrows, 1985

Canadian Wildlife and Tourism Service. *Birdwatching: New Brunswick, Canada.* Fredericton: Tourism New Brunswick, 1985.

Cleveland, N.J., M.F. Murdoch, W.P. Neilly, and I.A. Ward. *Birder's Guide to Southeastern Manitoba.* Winnipeg: Minitoba Naturalist's Society, 1980.

David, N. *The Status and Distribution of Birds in Southern Quebec.* Club des Ornithologues de Quebec, 1980.

Dobson, Phyllis. *Where to Find Birds In Nova Scotia.* Halifax: Nova Scotia Bird Society, 1976.

Frisch, R. *Birds by the Dempster Highway.* Dawson City, Yukon: Dawson Museum.

Goodwin, Clive. E. *A Bird Finding Guide to Ontario.* University of Toronto Press, 1982.

James, R.D., P.L. McLaren, and J.C. Barlow. *Annotated Checklist of the Birds of Ontario.* Toronto: Royal Ontario Museum, 1976.

Jehl, J.R., and B.A. Smith. *Birds of the Churchill Region, Manitoba.* Winnepeg: Manitoba Musuem of Man and Nature, 1970.

Kreba, R. Field. *Checklist of Saskatchewan Birds.* Saskatchewan Museum of Natural History, 1983.

Mark, David M. *Where to Find Birds In British Columbia.* New Westminster: Kestrel Press, 1984.

Martin, K., and W. Cairns. *Avifaunal Survey of Prince Edward Island.* Canadian Wildlife Service, 1979.

Salt, W. Ray, and J. Salt. *The Birds of Alberta.* Edmonton: Hurting Publishers, 1976.

Scotter, G.W. *Birds of Nahanni National Park.* Northwest Territories, Saskatchewan: Natural History Society, 1985.

Squires, W.A. *The Birds of New Brunswick.* New Brunswick Museum Monograph Series, no. 7. 1976.

Periodicals

American Birds
National Audobon Society
950 Third Avenue
New York, NY 10022

Birder's World
720 E. 8th Street
Holland, MI 49423
Austin, TX 78765

Birding
American Birding Association
Box 4335

Bird Watcher's Digest
Box 110
Marietta, OH 45750

Canadian Birding
Site 14A, Box 43
RR #4
Armdale, NS B3L 4J4

The Living Bird Quarterly
Laboratory of Ornithology,
Cornell University
159 Sapsucker Woods Road
Ithaca, NY 14850

Nature Canada Quarterly
CNF
453 Sussex Drive
Ottawa, ON K1N 9Z9

WildBird Magazine
Box 57900
Los Angeles, CA 90057

Birdwatching Travel

Birding has become such a popular pastime that literally hundreds of travel agencies and touring companies specialize in birdwatching trips. Organized birding tours are available to easily accessible hotspots as well as the most remote locations. Birding tours differ from most "vacations" in that accommodations may be rather rustic and amenities may be minimal or nonexistent. But there are other benefits to "roughing it" in places like the Amazon rain forests.

Many Audobon societies sponsor birding trips, as do other environmental organizations. Some organizationa enlist the aid of volunteers for hands-on assistance in a multitude of research projects. The fee usually includes accommodations and meals; airfare may be a separate charge.

Flexibilty is the key to a successful birding excursion, especially when traveling into remote areas. Weather conditions, available transportation, communication, local facilities, and other factors can affect the most carefully laid plans.

Most travel companies offer brochures and/or catalogs of planned excursions. Contact them well in advance of your scheduled trip; some, especially those going to remote areas, have space limitations.

The following organizations can make your next vacation a memorable birding excursion:

United States

Alaska Discovery
Franklin Street
Juneau, AK 99801

Amazonia Expeditions
P.O. Box 499
Largo, FL 34649

Bush Masters
3117 Elm Avenue
Brookefield, IL 60513

Field Guiders Inc.
P.O. Box 160723-E
Austin, TX 78716

Las Ventanas De Osa Wildlife
  Refuge
P.O. Box 1089
Lake Helen, FL 32744

National Audobon Expedition
  Institute
Northeast Audobon Center
Sharon, CT 06069

Natural Habitat Wildlife Adventures
  P.O. Box 789
McAfee, NJ 07428

Canada

Federation of Ontario
  Naturalists
355 Lesmill Road
Don Mills, ON M3B 2W8

Birding Associations

United States

American Birding Association
Box 6599
Colorado Springs, CO 80934

American Ornithologists Union
National Museum of American History
Washington, DC 20560

Cornell Laboratory of Ornithology
159 Sapsucker Woods Road
Ithaca, NY 14850

National Audobon Society
950 Third Avenue
New York, NY 10022

Questers Worldwide Nature Tours
257 Park Avenue South
New York, NY 10010

Roger Tory Peterson Institute
110 Marvin Parkway
Jamestown, NY 14701

Victor Emanuel Nature Tours
P.O. Box 33008
Austin, TX 78764

Wilderness Birding Adventures
P.O. 10-3747T
Anchorage, AK 99510

Wildland Journeys
3516 N.E. 155th Street
Seattle, WA 98155

Wings
P.O. Box 31930
Tucson, AZ 85751

Canada

Canadian Nature Federation
453 Sussex Drive
Ottawa, ON K1N 9Z9

Club Ornithologues de Quebec
8191 de Zoo
Orainsville, PQ G1G 4G4

Federation of Ontario Naturalists
355 Lesmill Road
Don Mills, ON M3B 2W8

Ontario Field Ornithologists
Box 1204, Station B
Burlington, ON L7P 3S9

Society of Canadian Ornithologists
Provincial Musuem of Alberta
12845-102 Avenue
Edmonton, AB T5N OM6

INDEX